Suzanne Hadley Gosselin

FOREWORD BY DR. GREG AND ERIN SMALLEY

Expectant Parents

Preparing Together for the Journey of Parenthood

 TYNDALE HOUSE PUBLISHERS, INC.
CAROL STREAM, ILLINOIS

Expectant Parents
Copyright © 2014 by Focus on the Family

A Focus on the Family book published by Tyndale House Publishers, Inc., Carol Stream, Illinois 60188

Focus on the Family and the accompanying logo and design are federally registered trademarks of Focus on the Family, 8605 Explorer Drive, Colorado Springs, CO 80920.

TYNDALE and Tyndale's quill logo are registered trademarks of Tyndale House Publishers, Inc.

All Scripture quotations, unless otherwise indicated, are taken from the *Holy Bible, New International Version®*. NIV®. Copyright © 1973, 1978, 1984 by Biblica, Inc.™ Used by permission of Zondervan. All rights reserved worldwide (www.zondervan.com). Scripture quotations marked (ESV) are from *The Holy Bible, English Standard Version®*, (ESV®), copyright © 2001 by Crossway, a publishing ministry of Good News Publishers. Used by permission. All rights reserved.

The use of material from or references to various websites does not imply endorsement of those sites in their entirety. Availability of websites and pages is subject to change without notice.

All stories in this book are true and are used by permission. In some cases, people's names and certain details of their stories have been changed to protect the privacy of the individuals involved. However, the facts of what happened and the underlying principles have been conveyed as accurately as possible.

Editor: Brandy Bruce
Cover photograph copyright © Gus Dizon. All rights reserved.
Cover design by Jacqueline L. Nuñez

Library of Congress Cataloging-in-Publication Data
Gosselin, Suzanne Hadley.
  Expectant parents / By Suzanne Hadley Gosselin. — First Edition.
    pages cm. — (A focus on the family book)
  Includes bibliographical references and index.
  ISBN 978-1-58997-794-5 (alk. paper)
  1. Parenting—Religious aspects—Christianity. 2. Parents—Religious life. 3. Marriage—Religious aspects—Christianity. 4. Pregnancy—Religious aspects—Christianity. I. Title.
  BV4529.G68 2014
  248.8'45—dc23
                                    2014011848

Printed in the United States of America
1   2   3   4   5   6   7   8   9 /19   18   17   16   15   14

To Kevin, my husband, best friend, and biggest fan. God gave me such a good and perfect gift in you. And to my children, Josiah, Sadie, and Amelia. God has used you to teach me about grace; you fill my days with love and bring me more joy than I thought possible.

CONTENTS

FOREWORD

You're about to become parents! Congratulations! We are guessing this is something most of you have dreamt about your entire life—or maybe becoming a parent is bringing up some mixed emotions for you. Everyone is different in their initial reaction to hearing the words "You're pregnant." We are convinced that pregnancy is ten full months so we can process, prepare, and plan for becoming a new parent.

We are sure many of you have already heard, "Everything is about to change." This may have been said in a positive light or maybe a negative one. We can remember walking out of our first Lamaze class and thinking, *What have we gotten ourselves into?* We can honestly say now, after having three biological children and one through the gift of adoption, "Yes, everything does change." But we can assure you, becoming parents set us on a wonderful, delightful, challenging journey—one that we would not change for the world. However, the only way we know to encourage you on this journey is to emphasize the need to be a "lifelong" learner. Educate yourself in each new season—especially the one you are about to embark on!

I (Erin), as a former labor and delivery nurse, have thought back to the number of babies and parents I escorted out the door of the hospital, knowing that I never asked them one question about their marriage, who was going to be caring for the infant, how this has impacted their relationship, and so on. I know this from my own experience as well; they hand you the baby and you walk out the door, without an instruction manual! But when Greg and I were going through the adoption process (prior to receiving approval to adopt our Annie), I was amazed by how much we were asked about not only our marriage, but our parents' marriages, our plan for caring for an adopted child, and the list went on and on! The preparation time actually gave us an opportunity to really talk through the changes and challenges before us, and that was a good thing.

I (Greg) was struck with what a need there is for a book just like *Expectant Parents*—a guide to thinking through how this child will impact you both individually, as well as your marriage. This book is filled with stories from real moms and dads who've been there; you'll find practical tips and advice as you prepare to dive into this adventure of parenting.

We are so excited you are taking advantage of all this book has to offer. We are confident that you will reflect back on the information, stories, and content you are about to experience. We couldn't put the book down once we started reading and found ourselves thinking, *We sure wish we would have had this book prior to bringing our first daughter home!*

Yes, life will change once your little one arrives. However, as you read this book, you're taking the first step to being well prepared for the changes that will come and for the incredible adventure and journey that lie ahead.

Blessings!
Dr. Greg and Erin Smalley

INTRODUCTION

My story is just one story.

Well, two stories, to be exact.

The first began on a rainy December day. That's when my first-born, Josiah Alexander, made his entrance, to the sweet strains of Christmas carols.

I "slow danced" with my husband for a good part of the day, my arms draped around his neck. I can still remember his eyes—the kind, steady eyes I'd fallen in love with two years earlier—focused on mine as we labored together. I think we both knew we stood at the threshold of an event that would change our lives forever.

When labor became painful, he stroked my hair and prayed for me. And when my wiggly boy, all arms and legs, was placed in my arms, all I could do was whisper, "I love you."

My second-born arrived twenty months later, on an August evening long after most people were in their beds. We had chosen not to find out the gender of our baby (so we could "do that once"), but we were convinced we were having another boy.

My water broke that morning, and we checked into the hospital a few hours later. At 5:00 PM, with no contractions in sight, labor was induced. I walked the halls for most of the evening, in labor but with barely perceivable contractions.

Then, suddenly, at 11:15—when I had been given the highest dose of Pitocin possible—hard labor began. (This time I preferred leaning over the bed, swaying and holding my husband's hands—to his relief.)

"Do you want the good news or the good news?" the nurse said after checking my cervix. "You're nine centimeters and fully effaced."

Our OB arrived at midnight; and our *daughter* was born at 12:16 AM.

Having only written down a few girl names arbitrarily, we named our daughter on the spot (after a brief, whispered conference). We named her Sadie Elizabeth, which means "Princess" and "My God Is an Oath."

Her name was fitting. During both births and our journey into parenthood, God has been our oath—our promise. Through the newness of being parents and the ups and downs of our son's medical problems, God's promise to be with us and care for us stood firm.

If you're reading this book, you are probably expecting your own little miracle. You are stepping closer to what is sure to be one of the most radical and sacred events of your life. Beyond the birth itself, you are about to embark on the astounding—and humbling—task of shepherding the soul of another. One who has been specifically entrusted to you.

My story is mine—unique from the others you will hear about in this book—sweet graces and details woven together by God. Plans dreamed up in His mind before time began. And your story is yours. It may share similarities with mine, or it may be completely different. But one thing will be the same. In the same way that God walked with Kevin and me as we traveled a path full of unknowns, He will be with you also. He has begun a good work in you and in the life of your child, which He has every intention to complete (see Philippians 1:6).

Your birth story will be exquisite. It will also be messy and awkward at times. There will be tears, laughter, pain, and unspeakable joy, all rolled up in one amazing bundle. You will encounter God's love and care in ways you never imagined. You will be stretched (in every way possible), and you will be filled with more love than you ever anticipated.

God already knows your birth story, every detail. And He will be with you every step of the way.

∞

If this is your first baby, you are probably excited—though at times anxious—about bringing a new little life into the world.

Will he look like you or your spouse? Will she have chubby cheeks or an abundance of downy soft hair on her head? What will his skin feel like? The excitement of a new baby has the tendency to inspire wonder and a special kind of joy.

My friend Kelly describes sneaking into the nursery days before her daughter's birth, and picking up the tiny outfits and pressing them to her nose.

"I would breathe in the smell of those little clothes," she says, "and dream of what it would be like when she was finally here. It seems silly now, but I was just so excited."

My own first pregnancy came after I had been single for many years and wondered if having a family would ever happen for me. When I became pregnant six months after getting married, waiting for the baby was like waiting for Christmas Day! (Literally, since my son was born on December 17.)

∞

Maybe your pregnancy was unexpected or happened sooner than anticipated, and you have some anxiety about what you've gotten yourself into. Or maybe you've waited and prayed for a baby for years, and similar to Sarah and Abraham in the Bible, for you, this child is the fulfillment of long-held desires and hopes. Perhaps the timing was exactly what you were hoping for, and you're confident that *now* is the perfect time to start a family.

Regardless of how you entered the journey of pregnancy, you are here. And I hope this book will provide you with encouragement, practical advice, and motivation to start out strong. More than that, I hope it will show you how to build a foundation of faith in your family from your child's earliest days.

If you're feeling some fear and apprehension, you're not alone. Almost all of the expectant parents I spoke with during the course of writing this book had fears and concerns, such as, Will the baby be healthy? Will my labor and delivery go as planned? What will work and finances look like after the baby comes? Will my relationship with my spouse change for the worse? How will pregnancy affect my body?

Within these pages, all of those questions will be addressed, and more. As you read, you will discover insights from other parents, advice from experts, discussion questions to deepen your relationship with your spouse, and even suggested activities to enrich your pregnancy and prepare you for parenthood.

You will also find some additional help in the appendices on various topics, including miscarriage, adoption, and welcoming a baby to a blended family.

My prayer is that this will be a truly meaningful and memorable season of life as you begin your family . . . and discover your story.

CHAPTER ONE

When Two Become Three

"Everything's going to change."

People seemed delighted to tell us this when they found out we were expecting for the first time. To my husband, Kevin, and me, these words seemed more like an ominous warning than the wondrous prediction I'm sure they were intended to be. The very idea of such a life-altering change stirred up resistance in my spirit. I knew things would change a little, of course, but certainly *everything* wouldn't change.

One thing I was confident would not change was my relationship with Kevin. He and I met in a fairy-tale fashion one Sunday evening (as he made my latte at Starbucks), and our courtship and marriage swiftly followed suit.

We both love children and were hoping to have a family, so six months into marriage, when we learned a baby would be joining us, we were overjoyed. We were also still solidly in the honeymoon phase. Though we had heard stories about how a baby changes things, I stubbornly refused to believe that pregnancy and the birth of a child would disturb our "perfect" marriage.

While not every couple starts a family as soon after marriage as we did, every couple will face their own relational adjustments as they negotiate the season of pregnancy and the one following the baby's arrival. Although God's plan for each couple and family is different, my belief that absolutely *nothing* would change in our marriage was . . . well, mistaken.

Not only were others intent on telling us that everything would change, but they were also fond of telling us their parental "horror stories." For example, they would recount the chilling tale of their thirty-eight-hour labor experience or Junior's epic blowout on the airplane.

Sleep in, they would tell us. Go to the late movie. Look deeply into one another's eyes, because those days are coming to an end . . . forever (or at least the next eighteen years). Soon the most interesting thing in your life is going to be the bodily fluids emerging from a being the size of a burrito. And before you know it, your greatest desire won't be for a tropical vacation or a new car but for an hour of uninterrupted sleep . . . or a shower.

Mercifully, those days will pass, the naysayers would continue, only to be replaced by years on end when you'll completely lose your own identity (particularly in the eyes of the child's grandparents, formerly known as your parents), your days will revolve around naptime (Baby's, not yours, unfortunately), and all your worldly goods will be systematically destroyed by your little "blessings" and/or permeated by Cheerios, raisins, or unidentifiable crumbs.

It's enough to panic any expectant couple. Like us, you may begin to wonder if all your former happiness as a couple is about to slip away.

What those well-meaning naysayers neglect to tell you is that *it's worth it*.

Let that sink in for a minute. *It's worth it.*

And as you follow the development of your little one inside the womb and plan for the joys of welcoming him or her, you are likely more in tune with the miraculous nature of parenthood than those in the throes of child rearing.

The truth is, the thrill you are experiencing as expectant parents is more in line with reality. And whether you feel it right now or not, you *will* be better off for having a child. Ask any parent you know: There are certain inalienable rights and joys that come along with being a mom or a dad.

Ashley, a mother of two, says, "There is absolutely no way—*zero*—that you can understand how much you will love your child until you have a child. It's the last great, unopened chamber of your heart that doesn't unlock until you have a baby. People can (and love to) tell you how hard it is to care for kids. They don't tell you enough about that secret, unopened chamber. They should."

So while things are going to change (and we're going to look at that in depth and offer tips on how to navigate the journey), let me assure you that entering into the adventure of parenthood is not the end; it's only the beginning. And it is *so* worth it.

WHEN BABY MAKES THREE

I went into pregnancy naïve about how the addition of a baby might affect Kevin's and my relationship. There was no way for me (or him) to anticipate how hormones, sleep deprivation, the stress of caring for an infant, and just adjusting to a *huge* life change in general would test our marital bliss. I'm thankful that we concentrated on good communication during pregnancy, which allowed us to anticipate, and prepare for, some of the challenges ahead.

When Dr. Greg and Erin Smalley learned they were pregnant with their first child, they weren't expecting to start a family for another five years. Though the birth of their daughter radically changed the couple's immediate plans for the future, "This pregnancy was not unknown to God," Erin says. "Our daughter was such an incredible blessing."

In addition to having to change their immediate plans—which included calling off a study-abroad opportunity in England—the couple says they also experienced a shift in their relationship. Dr. Smalley, author and vice president of Family Ministries at Focus on the Family, and his wife, Erin, a counselor and former labor and delivery nurse, identify three areas where expectant couples may experience changes in their relationship:

1. Communication. When a baby is on the way, a couple's conversation can become *all* about the baby. "You're preparing your home and relationship for this baby to join your family," Erin says. "Of course you're going to talk about it!"

This kind of conversation is healthy and natural, but couples should also be sensitive to what their partner needs.

"There's something magical and amazing about dreaming about parenthood together and deciding on names and thinking about who this child will be," Greg says. "But your spouse may also want to talk about other interests."

"You need to see yourself as a couple, not just a couple of parents," Erin adds. "That's something you'll need to do over the rest of your parenting years."

While it's important to remain sensitive to the needs of your spouse, there's no need to eliminate conversation about the baby altogether. Some of my best memories from my first pregnancy involve talking about the baby with Kevin, as well as special outings we took to the baby store and staying up until all hours of the night scouring baby-name websites.

As your topics of conversation expand to stroller brands and cloth or disposable, just make sure you're engaging your spouse in conversation that makes him or her feel loved and valued.

Gary's (and Lisa's) Date-Night Questions

by Gary Thomas, author of *Sacred Marriage*

Go out for dinner or coffee, and use these great questions to avoid making it all about Baby!

- If money wasn't an issue, what would be your dream vacation in the next ten years? With kids? Without kids?
- What is the one thing that is most frustrating about your life right now?
- How would you describe your ideal day off?
- What part of your day do you most look forward to? Why?
- What makes you feel closest to me as your spouse?
- How do you feel about the church we attend? Where is the best area to invest in our church family during this season of our lives?
- Let's imagine our child is grown and going through premarital counseling. The counselor asks him or her to describe our marriage. What do you hope he or she will say? What can we do to create a marriage like that?

Greg says listening—especially on the part of the guy—is key to good communication during pregnancy. "Men like to communicate when there's a problem to solve," he says. "When hormones are raging and it's hard to know if her feelings are rational, the worst thing I can do is debate whether her feeling is right or wrong. I'm going to be a listener."

2. **Care.** Pregnancy is a season where tenderness between partners can expand exponentially.

Not long ago, I was at the gym working out on an elliptical machine. A few minutes into my workout, a woman stepped onto the machine next to me, and not long after that, her husband came and stood next to her. He lingered there for the remaining twenty minutes of her workout, which I found a little strange.

Only after she finished did I notice the telling "bump" protruding from her middle and the signature pregnancy swagger as her husband accompanied her—his hand on the small of her back—to the watercooler. I smiled, remembering how attentive and protective my husband was during my pregnancies.

"Our perspective of each other changed," Greg says, recalling Erin's first pregnancy. "You find a new variation of your love for each other. I remember looking at Erin and watching her belly grow and thinking, *She's carrying my child. Wow.* I gained a whole new level of appreciation for who she was. There's an amazing beauty to your wife when she's pregnant with your child.

"And for a woman, having her husband take care of her and do chores that maybe he hasn't done before or work extra shifts to prepare for the expenses—all of that really adds to a deepening love for each other."

3. Conflict. It would be great if every relational change during the journey of pregnancy was a positive one, but with big changes ahead, new relationship difficulties can surface.

"Whether this baby will bring spouses closer together or drive them apart has everything to do with the pre-baby relationship," Greg says. "Having a child is going to intensify everything in the relationship. The good will be even better, but the bad will be magnified by 1,000 percent. When you factor in sleep deprivation, the hormones, the exhaustion, even tiny things spark. What may have been a small disagreement before can turn into a major issue."

Erin adds, "The couple may be dealing with some new frustrations with each other. There are a lot of women who assume that their spouse should know about and be meeting these new needs she has. Sometimes even the intense mood swings—the highs and lows of pregnancy—can lead to conflicts and disappointments that are new for a couple."

The Smalleys suggest that couples seek counseling for any significant issues that arise. "Shore up your relationship *before* the baby comes," Greg says. "How are you handling stress? How are you dealing with conflict? If there are any past issues you haven't dealt with, deal with them now."

In addition, he advises, "Keep short accounts. When conflict happens, give each other space, the benefit of the doubt, and grace. Be quick to offer forgiveness."

View from the Nursery

by Jennifer DeBrito

When I was pregnant with my son, it seemed like everything I read contained the message that my husband should be spoiling me rotten.

I was really hopeful for a special gift from him at my baby shower, or a nice little getaway at some point during my pregnancy. When neither of those things happened, I expected that he'd at least give me a gift the day our son was born. That also did not happen.

All these expectations I had (which he knew nothing about because he hadn't read any of the books or magazines that gave me these ideas) led to disappointment and hurt feelings.

I later realized that if I had never read those books and

magazines, I probably would not have expected the grand gestures I was hoping to receive. My husband hadn't intentionally let me down; the problem was my expectations.

Looking back seven years later, I am able to see all the things my husband did for me that I overlooked.

He took me to every garage sale in town until I found the perfect baby furniture, and then he carefully cleaned and set up every last piece so the nursery would be ready. He attended childbirth classes with me after very long days at a job he didn't enjoy. He cleaned the bathrooms for the duration of my pregnancy to protect me and the baby from harsh chemicals. He rubbed my feet daily and even went shopping for maternity clothes with me (twice!).

No wonder he seemed upset when I complained that he hadn't done anything for me! He had supported me and offered kindness after kindness, but I was too wrapped up in my own expectations to take notice.

If I could change anything from my pregnancies, I would recognize the extra time, attention, and effort my husband gave for the gifts they truly were.

STAYING CONNECTED DURING PREGNANCY

While many couples will experience a deepening of their relationship through their shared anticipation of Baby-on-the-Way, pregnancy can also be a time when a couple drifts apart slightly. In the past, it's been "just the two of us." Now the wife's mind may be focused on the baby growing inside her and how her life is about to change, while the husband's daily routine continues on much the same. (Except maybe for those late-night grocery runs to satisfy pregnancy cravings.)

There are many things couples can do to foster togetherness during this season. Think about the things you would like to do, "just the two of you," and do them—kind of a pre-baby bucket list.

My first pregnancy was very romantic; Kevin and I traveled, attended childbirth classes together, and went on some special dates (one of them to celebrate our first anniversary!). We tried to be intentional about celebrating the closing of the chapter of "just us."

Another way to minimize conflict, Greg says, is to avoid making other major life decisions during pregnancy. "Try not to change jobs, make a major move, or even buy a home," he says. "There's such an enormous amount of stress as you're preparing for the baby. Be cautious about adding more."

The "Babymoon"

A fun way to connect as a couple before the arrival of your baby is to take a "babymoon"—a getaway with your spouse to enjoy some romance and downtime before the baby comes. This vacation can be a memorable experience as you savor your last days exclusively as a couple.

For our babymoon, Kevin and I drove to a mountain town five hours away and stayed at a bed-and-breakfast. We spent a few days exploring the local attractions, dining in cute eateries, and enjoying one another's company in a calm, beautiful environment.

If finances are tight, plan a simple overnight trip or even create a "getaway" feel at home. If you have a little more time and money, explore a new city. Much like your honeymoon, the babymoon can be a time for enjoying one another and dreaming about the future.

Here are a few ideas to make the most of your babymoon:

Pamper. Plan a luxury or two, such as a romantic dinner, hotel room service, a couple's massage, or a pedicure.

Pictures. Take photos; it will be fun to look back on the special times you shared together preceding your baby's birth.

Plan. Keep your schedule light and leave lots of space for quiet time and impromptu naps. At fourteen weeks pregnant, I began to cry when Kevin encouraged me to continue on an easy uphill hike. A feat that normally would have been easy for me was just too exhausting and sparked an emotional spill. We took a drive through the mountains instead.

Primp. Purchase a new outfit, clothing item, or accessory to make you feel lovely and remind you of your special getaway. This doesn't just have to apply to Mom, either. Something new can make Dad feel special, too.

MAKING YOUR MARRIAGE A PRIORITY

With parenthood just around the corner, now is a good time to decide together how you will make your relationship a priority. While your true goal will be to have a Christ-centered home, the marriage itself is a foundational, God-ordained block for the family.

Studies abound on the benefits for children of having parents engaged in a strong, loving marriage. In his article for *Scientific American Mind* in 2010, psychologist Dr. Robert Epstein revealed the results of a study he conducted with Shannon Fox. The study compared ten effective parenting practices and ranked them. The top result (the most effective parenting practice) was giving the child love and affection. However, the next two surprised Epstein: managing stress in the parent's own life and having a good relationship with his or her spouse.

"In other words, your children benefit not just from how you treat them but also from how you treat your partner and yourself," Dr. Epstein concludes. "Children benefit when their parents share a loving, affectionate relationship marked by forgiveness and respect."[1]

Joshua Rogers, writer and blogger at JoshuaRogers.com, makes another important point on the impact of the husband-wife relationship in a blog post he wrote upon the birth of his second daughter:

> As I ponder the life ahead for my two-day-old daughter, it hits me all over again: If I'm going to be a good dad, I've got to be a good husband first. Because whether I like it or not, my daughters will look at the way I love their mother, and it will teach them what kind of man they deserve.
>
> Think of it—I'm going to be the first man my daughters love, and I will set the precedent as to how a man should treat a woman. If I am respectfully direct when I communicate with their mom, they will probably avoid a passive-aggressive man who gives them the cold shoulder. If I criticize and pick at their mom, they will tolerate a man who puts them down. But if I strive to love, serve, honor, and cherish their mom, they will look for the qualities of Christ in a man.[2]

Keeping your marriage strong in the midst of the chaos of caring for a baby may seem like a daunting, or even impossible, task. Don't worry. Throughout this book, we're going to consider practical ways to help your marriage thrive not only during pregnancy but also in the seasons to follow. This foundational element of your family is so important, and with God's help you *can* do this! The first step, however, is deciding together that you're going to make your marriage a priority.

It's no secret that a thriving sexual relationship is a key component to a strong marriage. Some couples may experience great sex during pregnancy, while others may discover that pregnancy symptoms put a damper on bedroom activities. Similarly, for some couples, resuming intimacy after the baby arrives comes easily and naturally, while others may face some obstacles. Either way, psychologist and author Dr. Juli Slattery says couples need to be proactive about sex, both during pregnancy and following the baby's birth.

As co-founder and president of Authentic Intimacy, a Christian organization that ministers to women on topics related to intimacy in marriage, Dr. Slattery has spoken to many couples about making time for intimacy even during this time of transition.

> ROMANCE TIP:
> Try making the first time special by going on a special date, creating a romantic atmosphere, and minimizing distractions.

"There's a balance between saying, 'This is a tiring stage of life, and we can't put as much energy into sex as we did before the baby'—that's just a reality—and putting it on the back burner, saying, 'We'll get to it someday.' You have to make sex a priority."

While the following suggestions relate to bringing back intimacy following your baby's birth, they are helpful to keep in mind during pregnancy as well.

Pay attention to one another's physical needs. The man will likely be ready for sex before the woman is. I heard of one husband who circled the six-week date on the calendar (and I'm sure many husbands are well aware of that magical day). While the man may be raring to go, the woman may feel the opposite. Combine what she's been through physically with post-pregnancy hormones, and she may be finding it difficult to "get in the mood."

"The mother is full of oxytocin, which creates a strong infatuation with her baby," Gary Thomas says. "She's bonding with her child, which is healthy, but she may be neglecting to do that with her husband. Some husbands can feel like their wives are having an 'affair' with the baby."

A woman can be sensitive to her husband by seeking to meet his sexual needs (once she is physically and emotionally able). And a man can be sensitive to his wife by waiting patiently until she is ready for sex while helping provide for some of her greatest needs, such as sleep, food, and relief from full-time care of their infant.

Sandra and Jake had been married for just a little over a year when their baby arrived. "I wanted to be sure we kept the newlywed flame alive," Sandra says. "Before the six weeks were up, we took showers together and tried other ways of being intimate. Not only did I feel like I was encouraging my husband, who was going through a big transition himself in becoming a dad, but it actually made me more excited for when we could start having sex again."

Make privacy a priority. While couples may choose to implement different practices for where the baby sleeps, protecting intimacy by creating a secluded area for Mom and Dad to be together is crucial. "We chose not to have our babies share our room or our bed with us," says Mary. "So we didn't struggle with privacy." Parents who choose to keep the baby in their room may consider placing the baby's bassinet in an area away from the bed. One couple moved the bassinet into their walk-in closet for small periods of time to create a feeling of privacy. Couples can also indulge in baby-free snuggle time, while the baby is sleeping or in the swing.

Make time for sex—schedule it if you have to! Dr. Slattery recommends that couples schedule sex at least one or two times a week (if they're not already having intercourse that frequently). "For a woman to enjoy sex, she has to be mentally and physically into it," Dr. Slattery explains. "It can feel like a marathon to take care of a baby all day and then immediately go into wanting to have sex. Choose a time based on the woman's schedule and energy level, as well as a time when you're most likely to not be interrupted." (Hint: This time may not be at the very end of the day when you are both exhausted.)

Jenna says that after having a baby, it took her a long time to get back into the mood for sex. "My hormones were crazy, and I felt like my body was no longer mine and my breasts were for the baby," she says. "At night I would lie in bed, stiff as a board, wondering if Chris wanted to have sex. I wouldn't relax until I heard him breathing and knew he was asleep. We went through a season of scheduling sex because that's what I needed. Scheduling let me relax on our nights off and build up to it on our nights 'on.' It took the fun, spontaneous nature out of it, but it was just for a season, and it worked for us."

Mary says, "I secretly set a goal for myself to initiate sex with my husband once a week. I would choose a day and think about it, beginning in the morning, to help prepare me for the night. By the time I put the baby to bed, I would be more than ready."

If you're finding it difficult or uncomfortable to have sex, seek medical attention. Dr. Slattery says, "Intercourse can be painful for some women, not just because of childbirth, but also because of the hormones involved in childbirth." Feeling some discomfort during the first few weeks after you resume intercourse is normal, she says. However, some women may develop a condition where the vaginal muscles tense up involuntarily and cause sex to be painful. A doctor can diagnose and treat most physical conditions that cause persistent pain during intercourse.

In a small percentage of women, childbirth can also bring up emotional trauma associated with past sexual abuse, rape, or abortion. Dr. Slattery suggests being proactive about seeking treatment for any physical or emotional conditions that arise so you and your spouse can get back to having sex regularly.

KEEP YOUR HEAD IN THE GAME

Despite the many joys of welcoming your bouncy bundle of joy, if your relationship feels a whole lot harder once the baby arrives, don't panic.

I was astounded by how needy and weepy I became during the first few weeks of parenthood (probably due in large part to post-pregnancy hormones). There were days when I felt extremely unlovable and ungrateful. Although the early trials of sleepless nights, out-of-control hormones, and feeling like a prisoner in my own home passed, new challenges replaced them. And I can't say it ever got easier, exactly. (I did get more proficient at dealing with those eight poopy diapers a day, though.)

During the relational lows of parenthood, it's important to remember that spiritual forces are at work. In *Devotions for a Sacred Marriage,* Gary Thomas writes:

> A married couple's relationship is the inner fortress in a cosmic spiritual battle. That fortress is not limited to just a man and woman; it also protects the children who result from that union. Even more than that, it protects generations of grandchildren and great grandchildren who will be influenced by their ancestors.
>
> With so much at stake, can we afford to be lackadaisical? Dare we forget that a powerful, pernicious being has made it his aim to wreck what God is trying to build? Even worse, are we cooperating with his agenda? By our actions, whether physical (flirting with an office mate, viewing pornography, getting so busy you have little or no time to work on your marriage)

or spiritual (refusing to forgive, holding a grudge, neglecting to build spiritual intimacy), are we foolishly and recklessly putting our marriage at risk?[3]

As believers we should not be surprised when our marriage relationships hit rocky terrain—especially around the birth of a child. This sacred relationship is a prime target for the enemy, who is "looking for someone to devour" (1 Peter 5:8), because he knows that destroying a marriage destroys a family. Crucial to keeping our marriages strong is maintaining intimacy, even when life changes come.

BETTER THAN EVER

Adding a baby to your family *will* change your relationship. But with good communication and attention to one another's needs, that change can actually strengthen and deepen your marriage.

"Get closer to God than you ever have been before," Gary Thomas suggests. "You need more grace, kindness, the servant heart of Jesus, strength, and discernment than ever before. Step up your marriage. Don't just stay married—stay connected."

Joshua Rogers says his biggest advice for new parents is this:

Whatever happens, take care of your marriage after you have a baby. When you're in the midst of nursing, swaddling, changing diapers, and rocking a baby to sleep, it seems like those things are the most important in the world—you feel like your baby is going to fall behind the rest of humanity unless you get it right. People tell themselves that they will take care of their marriage when things slow down.

But here's the thing: Life doesn't really slow down that much. Your baby grows up, becomes needy in new ways, and then you have more kids that multiply the demands children place on you. And having a messed-up nursing schedule isn't the thing that could damage your kid for life—it's having a mom and dad with a messed-up marriage.

My belief that nothing would change in our marriage when Kevin and I had a baby may have been mistaken. But the richness and joy added to our marriage relationship through having children is impossible to describe. It does take more effort to keep passion burning hot. But the effort is well worth it—for us and for our children.

TIME TO TALK

- On a scale of one to ten, how do you feel your marriage is weathering pregnancy?
- What do you feel your primary needs are right now? Discuss them with your spouse.
- What is something you would like to do—"just the two of you"—before the baby arrives?
- What are some ways you can make your home a marriage-centered home?
- How do you plan to keep passion and sex alive in your relationship once the baby comes?

Set aside some quiet time as a couple to talk about your relationship and the reasons you are thankful God brought you together. Pray and ask God to bless your marriage as you take on your new role as parents.

CHAPTER TWO

Hormones, Cravings, and Weight Gain, Oh My!

By now you (and your spouse) are probably familiar with some of the common pregnancy symptoms—fatigue, morning sickness, frequent trips to the restroom, cravings. But the physical experience of carrying a baby for nine months can go far beyond that. Here are a few less-common "symptoms" women have reported:

- The urge to eat a burrito once a day throughout the entire pregnancy
- Leg pain
- Extreme indecisiveness
- Aversion to chocolate
- Motion sickness while playing video games
- Loss of hair growth on legs (with boy pregnancies only)
- Excessive burping
- Crying while ordering food at a drive-through (happy cry)
- Crying while a co-worker eats fragrant pork (sad cry)
- Placing (and leaving) the telephone in the refrigerator
- Watching two complete seasons of *The Muppet Show* with no recollection of the event.

While you can expect some of the tried-and-true pregnancy symptoms (or, who knows, you may experience hardly any symptoms at all), you can also expect that your experience will be one of a kind. No new, strange feeling, urge, or reaction is off-limits. (I cried while watching insurance commercials.) At the same time, there are a few common symptoms for which you can prepare.

FIRST TRIMESTER

Morning sickness—a symptom shared by up to 90 percent of pregnant women—usually appears by the sixth week. This nausea, sometimes accompanied by vomiting, typically subsides between weeks thirteen and sixteen. For a small number of women, morning sickness continues throughout the pregnancy. (Also, morning sickness can occur at different times of day for different women.) Along with morning sickness, other early pregnancy symptoms include back pain, breast tenderness, constipation, frequent urination, and a heightened sense of smell.

SECOND TRIMESTER

At week thirteen, when the second trimester begins, most women get over morning sickness. This trimester is known as the "honeymoon period" of the pregnancy, as the nausea disappears and most women experience renewed energy. When I was four months pregnant with my son, I remember taking a six-mile hike in high-altitude Estes Park, Colorado. Apart from having to stop for an awkward pit stop behind some rocks, I had no problem completing the hike with even greater endurance than my in-laws.

Some symptoms that may occur during the second trimester include abdominal aches and pains (a result of the uterus growing and stretching out the ligaments) and increased breathlessness as the uterus grows and crowds the lungs. You will also begin to feel the baby move between the twelfth and twenty-second week. This sensation is known as "quickening." It is common for a mom not to notice the quickening as early if it is her first pregnancy.

Counting Kicks

Around the twenty-eight-week mark of your pregnancy, your doctor will suggest that you begin tracking your baby's movements or "kicks." Changes in your baby's movements may help identify potential pregnancy problems before the baby's heart rate is affected. It can also be a special bonding time for parent and baby.

Here are instructions to "kick-start" your routine:[1]

- Once a day, count the time it takes for your baby to make ten movements, such as a kick or roll. (Hiccups are not considered movements.) Your baby should move ten times in less than two hours (it usually takes about thirty minutes).
- Count kicks every day around the same time. Choose a time when your baby is normally active, such as after a snack or meal.
- Sit with your feet up or lie on your side. Count each of your baby's movements as one "kick." Count until you reach ten movements.
- If your baby has less than ten movements in two hours, or shows a sudden change in movements, call your doctor immediately.

By the twenty-first week of my pregnancy, I was beginning to worry that I hadn't yet felt my baby moving. Then one afternoon, I was working at my desk and felt that little "popcorn" sensation. I remember sending an excited text message to my husband to alert him of the event!

THIRD TRIMESTER

By the third trimester, you may be growing weary of being pregnant. This is when women complain of being the most uncomfortable. Fatigue, back pain, heartburn, frequent trips to the bathroom (particularly if Baby is resting on your bladder), and sleeplessness are common symptoms during the final days of pregnancy.

The good news is: You're almost there! The excitement of the impending birth will likely give you an emotional boost as you endure some of the more uncomfortable moments of carrying your baby.

During my third trimester, my husband and I went to a lot of plays and movies—places where I could sit comfortably while we enjoyed our final days of just being a couple.

FEELING GREAT

While some women experience a good deal of discomfort during pregnancy, others report feeling better than ever. "I felt the best I have my whole life while I was pregnant," says my friend Lisa. "I slept better, and my skin looked great."

There's also more for husbands to enjoy during pregnancy. Here are a few pregnancy "symptoms" you both might enjoy:

Longer hair, stronger nails. Hormonal changes in pregnant women, along with the benefits of those prenatal vitamins, can promote fingernail growth and lead to thick, shiny hair.

Enlarged breasts. As your milk ducts fill in preparation for feeding the baby, your breasts will grow noticeably larger. While you may enjoy filling out some feminine blouses, no doubt your husband will be the biggest fan of this change.

Glowing skin. Pregnant women are often described as having "the glow." An increase in blood volume can cause a fresh, natural blush on a pregnant woman's face. While some moms-to-be may experience pregnancy acne, clearer-than-usual skin is just as likely.

No periods. This one's a given. Enjoy at least nine menstruation-free months (more if you're breast-feeding) with no need for any pregnancy prevention measures. This comes in handy since many women report experiencing greater sensitivity and enjoyment of sex while pregnant.

FIGHTING THE BODY BLUES

While pregnancy has its perks, the physical changes can also take their toll. At a women's retreat, I once heard a female comedian lament the "body changes" brought about by childbearing and breast-feeding. As she described body parts that hung to the floor and issues involving bladder control, the older women around me laughed . . . a little too hard. One woman elbowed me and said, "You don't even have to breast-feed, sweetie. Being pregnant is enough." She must have seen the terror-stricken look on my face from all that I'd just heard, because she added, "It's totally worth it, of course."

Easy for you to say, I thought.

The message that pregnancy is a liability to a woman's body is prevalent. A few months before I became pregnant, a nationally known personal trainer gave an interview in which she claimed she would never get pregnant because she didn't want to ruin her body. I'm a bit ashamed to say it, but I spent more time worrying than I should have about whether pregnancy would "ruin" my body.

Living in a culture that places a lot of value on fitness and a particular standard of beauty (thin in most of the places that blossom during pregnancy) can make facing drastic and sudden body changes more than a little scary. If you're a woman, you may have already asked yourself some of these questions: "Will I gain a lot of weight that I won't be able to lose? Will my breasts lose their shape? Will I end up with ugly stretch marks or a scar? Will my husband still find my body attractive? Will *I* still find my body attractive?"

View from the Nursery
My Pretty Lines
by Emily Wagner

One day as I was getting out of the shower, my two-year-old daughter asked a question I was not prepared for: "Mama, what are those lines on your tummy?"

In a matter of moments, my mind darted from feelings of shame to dread at having to answer to realizing that neither of those emotions should motivate my response. The Lord and I had a brief conversation during which He whispered to me of the beauty inherent in the creation of life.

Though I didn't realize it at the time, the response He gave me for my precious, inquisitive daughter would be transformative for both of our views on beauty.

"Those are the lines where Mama's tummy stretched to make room for you and Sissy to grow there. Aren't they beautiful?"

Beautiful. Up until that moment, that is not a word I would have used to describe my stretched, baggy, scarred stomach. But I suddenly realized that's exactly what it was.

Somehow, within my womb, two little girls came into being and grew until the time came for them to join the world. Nothing about that process can be considered anything but beautiful. True, there was pain in the process—physical pain and emotional pain—but the end result was life. Why should I feel any shame in bodily changes that yielded two amazing little girls?

When my daughter asked her question, she wasn't attempting to point out my deficiencies; she merely noticed something about my body that she hadn't noticed before and wondered what it was. To her, my stretch marks and C-section scar were part of what she associates with womanhood and motherhood, both of which she aspires to with all the daydreaming of a typical little girl.

In that moment, I was given the opportunity to either communicate dissatisfaction with motherhood or joy in it. And, through the Holy Spirit's prompting, I communicated joy—even in one of my least favorite parts of being a mother.

She doesn't always notice my stretch marks these days, but when she points them out, it's with words like, "I love your pretty lines, Mama."

My pretty lines.

That's what they are: beautiful reminders of the joys and terrors, the difficulties and triumphs of birthing children. May I daily embrace all that God has given me, the pleasant and the not-so-pleasant, knowing that my body is a temple that I am called to care for and use, not for my own glory, but for the glory of the Lord.

The good news is, for most women, these physical changes are relatively minor and temporary—especially after the first baby. Dr. Kevin Weary, who has been an OB-GYN for seventeen years, says, "While it is quite possible Mom will add a new 'maternal beauty mark' or two from pregnancy, the extreme changes many women fear are very unlikely for the majority of women."

In addition, he points out that these changes are extremely normal and natural. "God has designed these earthly vessels to change with time and with different stages of life," he says. "Most men I know don't view these changes to their wives' bodies as unattractive—rather, quite the opposite."

Let me talk to the guys again. (I know you've probably been skimming some of the last few pages, and that's okay.) It's likely you not only find your wife's bodily changes acceptable—you find them attractive. *Tell her!* She needs to hear it. One of the top ways for a woman to feel lovely during pregnancy is to hear often from her husband that she is beautiful.

Alex, dad of six-month-old Owen, reports that he and his wife, Laura, made the process fun by taking a weekly picture of her growing baby bump. "We took a photo of her each week standing in the same position," he says. "It was great to flip through the photos at the end and see the slow change. It's such a unique and amazing time of life for a woman to have the opportunity to carry a little life inside her for nine months!"

Joshua says he didn't really notice his wife's gradual physical changes until someone would point it out. "We were at the store one night," he says, "and the male cashier, who was probably in his early twenties, looked at my wife's stomach in awe and said, 'Oh my gosh, I hope you're pregnant with twins.'"

While such comments may be funny to look back on later, they may not be humorous in the moment. Erin Smalley says she remembers a few hurtful comments she received about her early pregnancy weight gain. "Those comments can cut to the core when you're not comfortable with your body," she says. If you're feeling down about your pregnancy shape, she suggests these steps to beat the body blues:

Embrace it. We come in all shapes and sizes, and pregnancy affects each of us differently. As a labor and delivery nurse, I saw thousands of pregnant women, and each of them looked different, yet not one of them was *not* beautiful. They were all beautiful in their own way.

Do something about it. Be good to yourself. Take care of yourself emotionally and physically. Part of pregnancy is listening to your body.

Talk about it. If you're struggling with how you look and are feeling uncomfortable with the amount of weight you've gained, talk to your doctor. Focus on having a healthy diet and staying active with your doctor's approval.

Be amazed by it. Your body is being used as an incubator for a human life! That's pretty amazing.

The days immediately following the baby's birth can also be disheartening when it comes to your body. Good news: You lose between fifteen and twenty pounds, on average, just by giving birth! Bad news: You likely gained more than twenty pounds, and your body doesn't look exactly the same as it did pre-pregnancy.

I remember looking at my stomach the day after I gave birth and being shocked at what looked like a large, deflated balloon. (Thankfully, it went back to a normal, less-frightening shape within a few weeks.)

My friend Kristina told me that in those first few months after her baby was born, it helped her to focus on the positives of her body. "I remember feeling a bit self-conscious about my pudgy, saggy, baggy tummy," she says, "but my breasts were amazing! Focusing on that made me feel more beautiful."

Dad Extras

How to Affirm Your Wife during Pregnancy

Adapted from *The Deliberate Mom*[2]

Hey, guys, if you've been tuning out some of this physical stuff, here's what you need to know. Check out some simple ways you can support your wife during pregnancy and beyond.

1. **Understand.** You can support your wife by taking the time to learn what kinds of physical changes she is experiencing and how the baby is developing. Many smartphone apps provide this information on a daily or weekly basis.

2. **Listen.** Your wife always needs your listening ear, but now more than ever. Listen to her woes. Sympathize with her worries. Sincerely listen and *hear* what she is saying.

3. **Help.** There's no better time to run the vacuum cleaner, wash the dishes, do the laundry, or even make an occasional dinner. Your wife is tired and will be uplifted by your willingness to serve.

4. **Be at her beck and call.** If she's craving a grape slushie when it's minus-ten degrees outside, don't try to talk her out of her craving. Drive around town to find her the perfect slushie. Trust me, these are memories in the making; you'll laugh about them later.

5. **Up the enthusiasm.** If your wife is ecstatic about a birthing or parenting class, try your best to share in her excitement. Even if you have to fake your enthusiasm, do it! To her, your lack of excitement equals lack of excitement about the baby or her.

6. **Be romantic.** She needs to know you love her, pregnant or not. An extra show of romance can help smooth over her rough days and emotional moments. Give her a greeting card expressing your love, slow dance in the living room, bring her a bouquet of flowers, or put together a sappy slide show.

7. **Help her relax.** A number of physical and emotional stresses accompany pregnancy. Find ways to help your wife relax. Prepare a candlelight bubble bath or give her a shoulder or foot rub. You may even want to schedule a prenatal massage shortly before Baby's arrival.

8. **Treat her.** Arrange for some professional housecleaning, treat her to a manicure or pedicure, or take her to the mall and let her choose a stylish maternity outfit.

9. **Remind her that she's beautiful (inside and out).** Your wife may be feeling frumpy. Remind her of all the things you love and adore about her.

10. **Help her nest.** Make things easier on your wife by painting, cleaning, shopping for baby gear, and putting together nursery furniture.

PREGNANCY HORMONES

At no other time, with the exception of puberty, will a woman's body be so overrun with hormones than during pregnancy. From human chorionic gonadotropin (hCG), which caused the positive on your pregnancy test, to estrogen and oxytocin, a pregnant woman's body is awash with hormones during pregnancy, labor, and in the weeks following birth.

Hormones can do everything from cause morning sickness and

pregnancy acne to bring on cravings and heightened emotions. Many women report that hormones make them feel irrational or "out of control."

Brandy says she experienced a lot of hormonal ups and downs with both of her pregnancies, including postpartum depression (more on postpartum depression in Appendix III). "With my first baby, I was just weepy a lot and on edge," she says. "Don't get me wrong, I was *thrilled* to be pregnant, but I cried a lot."

She says her feelings were akin to having PMS for months on end. "I came to realize you really can't control your hormones," Brandy says. "They just get out of whack, and you come across as a weepy, crazy woman!"

To tread the emotional waters, Brandy sought out the help of friends and relatives. She says her husband, Jeff, was also a great source of comfort and support. "The main thing he did was just be there for me, even when I was emotionally unstable, and he had no idea what to do." Brandy's doctor monitored her postpartum depression until eventually the pregnancy-related hormones ran their course.

WHEN THINGS GET COMPLICATED

Complications are another physical aspect of pregnancy. When Kimi was informed (during her first pregnancy) that her baby was experiencing intrauterine growth restriction (IUGR), she says, "The future of my baby felt up in the air." Other than feeling sick, Kimi's pregnancy had been going smoothly. But at her thirty-two-week checkup, she learned the baby was measuring small. An ultrasound revealed that he was below the tenth percentile.

Although the doctor didn't seem overly concerned, Kimi was told that if the baby showed any signs of distress or dropped below the fifth percentile, she would have to deliver immediately.

"It was incredibly scary," she says. "I felt helpless. Nothing I could do would make the baby grow."

Pregnancy complications can put a real downer on an otherwise joyous season. Whether it's a minor abnormality that needs to be monitored or a more extreme condition requiring bed rest, complications add stress and anxiety to the pregnancy experience.

Although Kimi and her husband, Matt, were initially filled with anxious thoughts, they took one day—and one test—at a time. "I tried to be informed," Kimi says, "but not obsess over all the information available online."

Dr. Weary encourages couples to be cautious when researching on the Internet. "There is bad information," he says, "but there's also information that's accurate but extreme." Because people who have had negative experiences are more likely to write about them on the Internet than those who experienced positive outcomes, Dr. Weary says, "The information is definitely skewed to the bad stories."

Parents should also remember that the diagnosis of a complication doesn't necessarily mean there will be a negative outcome. "Just because we keep an eye on something doesn't mean it's going to be a problem," Dr. Weary says. "It just means we're going to watch you more closely."

Kimi, who experienced IUGR with all three of her pregnancies— and gave birth to three small but healthy babies—says she and Matt spent a lot of time praying together and talking about how they were feeling. "It does no good to blame yourself for things you can't control," she says. "Trust that God chose you to be this child's mother and that He will give you exactly what you need when you need it."

HEALTHY BEGINNINGS

The first time I ran while I was pregnant was also the last time I ran while I was pregnant. I had heard it could be done. And having run two half-marathons in my day, I figured I was a prime candidate to be *that* pregnant woman. You know, the one who works out consistently throughout her pregnancy and wears home a pair of pre-pregnancy jeans from the hospital.

Anyway, at fifteen weeks pregnant, after huffing and puffing through a mile on the treadmill, I gave up the dream. Other than a little walking and light hiking (when I felt like it), I didn't exercise regularly throughout that pregnancy.

Needless to say, I did not wear home pre-pregnancy jeans. Thankfully, I had been warned that not many women do. (In fact, the average woman should plan to wear home clothes she wore at six months pregnant.)

At my six-week follow-up appointment, my doctor encouraged me to start taking daily walks to improve my mood and get exercise. However, walking in the Colorado winter did not appeal to me in any way. I grew up in the rainy Pacific Northwest, where I was accustomed to holing up like a mole or a doomsday prepper throughout the winter months. And once my son was born, my favorite activities included— in no particular order—brewing a cup of decaf, keeping the blinds closed, flipping on the gas fireplace, blogging, snuggling my newborn, and watching movies.

And so I basically ignored the suggestion to exercise, assuming I'd get back into it in the summer months. That didn't happen. And when December rolled around again, and I became pregnant with my daughter, I was still carrying about fifteen extra pounds (not to mention the ten I'd put on since our wedding). Not the healthiest way to start a pregnancy. When all was said and done, I had between thirty and forty pounds to lose, and I lamented ignoring my doctor's advice.

For an optimum recovery, Dr. Weary encourages women to incorporate basic health habits as soon as possible after the baby's birth. "Try to eat healthfully, steal naps, and sleep when you can," he says. "Then, once you're through that four-to-six-week recovery period, add some physical activity. Exercise increases endorphins and raises serotonin levels, improving your mood."

He suggests that new moms start out by taking a thirty-minute walk three to five times a week, which, he says, can double as time for yourself. The benefits of exercise following pregnancy include greater energy, elevated mood, and weight loss. (See Appendix VIII for more on losing the baby weight.)

Husbands can support their wives as they drop the baby weight. Wes reports that his wife, Nica, who was in her twenties when she gave birth, returned to her pre-pregnancy weight naturally while breast-feeding. His experience was a different story. "I probably gained more weight in that first year than during the pregnancy," he admits. "I ate all of the same calories as Nica, because I love her. What else could I do?"

Alex, dad of a six-month-old, says he watches the baby in the morning so his wife can go to the gym to take a class. Arlene says her husband, James, supported her weight-loss goals by setting aside a "wardrobe fund" that she could use on new clothes once she met her goal. And new dad Austin rearranged the family budget so he could get his wife, Jennifer, a gym membership (with childcare), while he chose the free option of running for exercise.

Amber says the most meaningful way her husband, Mike, supported her in her after-baby fitness goals was by appreciating her womanly figure. "I'm still trying to lose the weight," she says, "but I don't have the baggage of worrying that my husband dislikes my current look. It frees me up emotionally to lose those pounds."

THE PREGNANCY SEASON

From cravings to cramps to complications, pregnancy has its highs and lows. But it's helpful to remember that your body is performing the miracle that God created it to do. Within your womb, God is crafting a new person, a new eternal soul.

Amber Bray Van Schooneveld, a contributor to *Where Moms Connect,* a ministry curriculum for moms, says, "When I was pregnant, I experienced a serious lack of perspective. I was so worried that I was getting fat and would never lose the weight, and I found it hard to remember that my pregnancy body was only for a short period of time and was so worth it.

"The biggest lesson I needed to remember was that life is full of seasons—a time to be a skinny teenager, a time to be a growing pregnant woman, a time to be a curvy and comforting mom.

"Culture tells us we need to rush out of these more mature seasons as quickly as possible, considering them a step backward from being a skinny teenager, but they're such a beautiful part of life and a beautiful privilege as a woman. Your body is in a different season during pregnancy and motherhood, and that's not just okay, it's beautiful."

Whether you love being pregnant or hate it—or fall somewhere in between—embrace the miracle of what God is doing in and through your body.

TIME TO TALK

- What symptoms or cravings have you experienced so far in pregnancy? (Write them down—some of them may be funny to remember later.)
- What can help you embrace the physical changes brought about by pregnancy?
- Talk to your spouse about how he can best affirm you during pregnancy.
- How will you prepare for and be proactive about the possibility of postpartum depression or the baby blues (a milder form)?

- How do you, as a couple, plan to implement basic health habits once the baby arrives? Think of some strategies, such as stocking up on healthy foods and deciding when and how you will exercise.

Take time to thank God for giving you a body that can conceive and bring a life into this world. Remember that most of the physical changes are temporary, and even those that aren't will be reminders of something sacred.

CHAPTER THREE

Being a Mom

Let's talk about motherhood for a few minutes. When Becky was pregnant with her first son, Carter, she was pretty sure she'd be a rock-star mom. "Not to brag," she says, "but I'd always wanted to be a mom, and I was the nurturing, caregiver type."

Not surprisingly, because of her personality and strengths, Becky took to mothering like a pro. During the next few years, two more little boys joined the family, and Becky continued to excel at being a mom.

"When they were younger, their needs were so doable," she says. "Feedings, naps, holding, snuggles . . . the needs felt so simple."

When it came to mothering infants and toddlers, Becky says she seemed to naturally anticipate what was wrong and what they needed. "I felt the usual range of emotions about whether or not I was using my gifts, talents, and education being at home with them, but overall I felt like I was born for this," she says.

Now, as her oldest son is entering middle school and the other two are in elementary school, Becky doesn't feel as confident. "The older they get, the more complex their needs are," she says. "They have deep, incommunicable needs involving ego, trust, and faith, and I scratch my head many times, wondering if I am able to be what they need as a mom."

As Becky presses on into the preteen years and beyond, she says, "Sometimes I long for the days where I felt competent and confident that even though I wasn't perfect, I was perfect for them. As they grow and mature, I am working harder than ever to really know my children and point them to a God who always 'gets them.'"

Julie's entrance into motherhood didn't go as smoothly as Becky's. As a twenty-nine-year-old media relations expert for a large nonprofit organization, she worked late one Friday night and had her daughter, Olivia, on Monday morning.

"It felt as though I was running seventy miles per hour, and then I ran off a cliff," she says. "I experienced a free fall and landed painfully."

When Julie first learned she was pregnant, she and her husband prayed about their future as a family, and she felt God was calling her to stay home with their daughter.

"I remember lying in bed one night, arguing with God about leaving my job," she says. "I knew He was asking me to stay home with my daughter, but I just didn't want to."

In an act of obedience and trust, Julie stayed home. She admits it wasn't easy at first. "My little one had colic, and I yearned for affirmation, but most of my social life had been linked to my job. I didn't feel like I fit into any moms groups; the women seemed like typical homemakers who were into things like sewing and crafts—things I wasn't good at and didn't enjoy."

A friend reminded Julie that every mom is different and perhaps she just wasn't "that kind of mom."

What eventually brought Julie joy in motherhood was falling in love with her daughter. "What gave me hope was seeing God use me in a new way," she says. "Ultimately, leaving my job began a long process of allowing God to strip me of my false identities so I could discover who I really am."

PREPARING FOR MOTHERHOOD

As you consider your own impending motherhood, you may feel a lot of confidence, like Becky. Or maybe, like Julie, you feel apprehension. To be honest, I started motherhood with a little of both.

When I was thirteen, as a young babysitter, I cared for a five-year-old, a three-year-old, and an eight-month-old three times a week. I was that responsible sitter who read the kids stories, played pretend games with them, and even cleaned the kitchen and dug crumbs out of the high chair. I figured when the time came, I'd be a pretty capable mom.

But while I imagined that day would come shortly after college, my singleness wore on for almost a decade following graduation. During that time, I adopted a different way of life. I developed a lifestyle that included ample free time, space to pursue my interests—such as running, travel, and improv comedy—and disposable income to indulge in some of the finer things of life.

Though I knew singleness was probably cementing my selfish tendencies (I only had myself to think about most of the time), I didn't see any way around it. Then I fell in love and married an accommodating man who shared my interests. My lifestyle didn't change much as we enjoyed grand adventures together.

Like Julie, I wasn't really prepared for the culture shock of quitting my job of ten years and staying home with an infant. Long gone were my babysitting days, and though I was delighted to have my dream of motherhood come true, I missed some things, and I struggled to adjust.

My friend Rochelle experienced something similar when her daughter was born. After more than twenty-five years of building her own routine and preferences, she worried she would be too "selfish" to be a good mom. She wondered how she would adjust to the body changes, sleep deprivation, less eating out, less money, and less time with friends.

"Ultimately, having a baby is the best thing ever," she says, "but in talking with other moms, I'm glad that I'm not alone in looking back longingly at the thirty-minute showers I used to take, the clothes I could wear, and not doing my makeup in my car—just for a few seconds of alone time."

Rochelle admits that sometimes she mourns the loss of freedom and the luxuries she used to have, "but one look at my little girl's face and it's forgotten," she says.

IMAGINING MOTHERHOOD

What do you picture when you think about being a mom and caring for an infant? Take a few minutes to write down how you picture the following after you become a mom:

- My outward appearance _____

- My daily activities _____

- My husband's involvement _____

- My relationship with my husband _____

- My social life _____

- My ideal day _____

Identify the areas you think will change significantly and those areas where you expect to see little to no change. What are your priorities?

As a new mom, I knew I wanted to take a shower, get dressed, and put on makeup (almost) every day. And I did. I wasn't willing to be one of those moms who didn't shower for days. And I was willing to sacrifice other things to make that happen. I also anticipated that my husband would be hands-on with the baby, which he was, sharing diaper duty and accompanying me to doctor's appointments when possible.

Dr. Greg Smalley says that it's important for husbands and wives to talk about their expectations for life after baby. "The problem with an expectation is that it is unknown," he says. "Either I'm unaware that I have an expectation or my spouse is unaware that I expect something. You want to bring these things into the light so you can both look at them and agree upon what is realistic."

His wife, Erin, adds, "These expectations may revolve around the roles your dad or your mom played. Those roles may be very different from what your spouse experienced. It's important to become aware of your expectations—what you're hoping for or expecting."

Here's an example of expectation drama. I grew up with a dad who left work promptly at 5:00 PM each day and came home to spend time with our family. Because of this example, I expected that Kevin would come home each night by 5:30 PM with rare exceptions.

Kevin grew up with a dad who worked long hours, often arriving home after 7:00 PM. Because of this, working thirty minutes to an hour late each night—without alerting me to the fact—didn't seem like a big deal to him. But it was to me.

Had we discovered the difference in our expectations before I was staying home with a baby (who inevitably became fussy and needy at exactly the same time I was trying to prepare dinner) and eagerly (desperately) anticipating my husband's arrival home each night, we could have avoided some relational stress and hurt feelings.

Using the list on the previous page as a starting point, discuss your expectations for motherhood with your husband. Find out what he imagines your life after Baby to look like. While the reality will probably not look exactly like either of you imagine, talking about your expectations can help you avoid disappointments and misunderstandings.

HOW NOT TO BECOME MOMZILLA

Maybe you've heard about women who become, well, a little scary when they have a baby. Like a mama bear, this woman becomes intensely focused on the welfare of her baby, excluding everything and everyone else—sometimes even the baby's father.

A woman I met at a moms group at church says she's particularly protective of her six-month-old because she delivered her . . . by herself . . . in the car (after not making it to the hospital in time). That mom has a pretty compelling reason to be a little overprotective. But most moms' reasons for becoming "Momzilla" aren't as obvious.

Dr. Juli Slattery explains that "hibernation" behavior is normal to a certain extent for new moms. "Motherhood is a huge adjustment," she says. "The mom is going to be insanely focused on the child. Some of that has to do with hormones and her insecurity in wanting to be a great mom. It's completely normal for her to kind of check out of everything else for about three months after she has the baby."

The truth is, being a mom of monstrous proportions often starts with attitudes formed before the baby ever arrives. With that in mind, how can you avoid becoming Momzilla? Here are a few common mistakes to avoid:

Excluding Dad. One of the biggest adjustments your husband will have to make is sharing you with the baby. This may even begin during pregnancy as you become more focused on your and the baby's needs. You can make this transition easier for him by including him in your pregnancy and when it comes to the baby's care. Although he may not always know exactly what to do or how to help, he wants to be involved in the process. Thanks to your exclusive nine months together and the hormones associated with childbirth (not to mention breast-feeding if you go that route), you have a head start on bonding with your baby.

You can help your husband bond with the new arrival by including him in decisions you make pre-baby and then entrusting him with some of the daily tasks of parenting a newborn.

"If sharing the parenting doesn't come naturally because you're staying home and he's working outside the home, you need to be intentional about inviting him into the parenting process," Dr. Slattery says. "As a new mom, I really struggled with this. My husband didn't always care for the baby the way I thought he should. If he stayed up during the night to feed the baby, he wouldn't follow the schedule. It drove me crazy. But I needed to learn that it was more important for my husband and me to share parenting tasks—and for him to feel confident as a dad—than it was for me to have him do everything the way that I thought it should be done."

My friend Kirsten and her husband, Nick, made an agreement before their daughter was born that he would change all the diapers during the first few weeks and take care of their daughter's bath time. This allowed him to have his "special time" with their daughter, and it provided a break for Kirsten.

Failing to accept help. When Kevin and I attended our childbirth class at the hospital, the instructor encouraged all of us new parents to consider allowing those eager relatives who had offered to come stay with us to do so. "And when your mother-in-law asks how she can help," she said, "have her take the baby after the middle-of-the-night feeding, change his diaper, and put him back to bed for you."

That advice sounded odd (and a little intrusive) to me at the time, but two babies later, I see her point. When we had our first child, Josiah, my sister and brother-in-law drove in from several states away. Not only did my sister attend the birth, she brought me a sandwich shortly after delivery (nothing ever tasted so good!), and she and her husband cleaned our house and made meals to last us a week. Coming home to a clean house stocked with tempting food was an incredible blessing and made our first week run smoothly.

Real Advice for New Parents

As women, we can easily get caught up in being the "perfect" parent and always doing the right thing. You can try to be that, but it's not what you were created for. You were created in God's image to be like Him. He gave you this child to show you your flaws, to say, "Oops" and "Will you forgive me?"

We need to show our kids our flaws so they know that we, and they, need a Savior. If I try to be the perfect parent, then my son will try to be the perfect child—when the thing God actually wants is to shine through us.

—*Sally, mother of two*

Likely you've had people offer to help you when the baby comes. Take them up on it! "The best thing for you and your new family is to accept help," Dr. Slattery says. "Let them run to the grocery store for you. Let them make dinner. Let them do your laundry." Although your first reaction may be to decline help, thinking you can handle it, allowing others to help out relieves a lot of the stress that comes with caring for a new baby.

Expecting perfection. New moms need to give themselves grace, Dr. Slattery says. "Lower your expectations. It's okay to have a messy house for a couple of months. It's okay to bring in take-out food. Don't expect much from yourself for the first few months."

My friend Grace remembers a time shortly after her daughter's birth where her self-sufficiency led to a meltdown. "A few days after our daughter's birth, we had to take our toddler to the doctor's for X-rays, which was a traumatic experience for all of us," she says. "When we got home, we had no food in the house, and we all were exhausted and hungry. I was in tears, feeling abandoned."

Grace's husband called his parents, who were in town visiting, to ask them to bring food and help put their toddler to bed for the night. "My pride was still not loving having to answer the door with a tear-stained face," Grace says, "but you can't expect others to just know you don't have food and need help. You have to ask."

Giving bad behavior a pass. As with anything stressful in life, having a new baby can become an excuse for treating others poorly. New moms, in particular, may struggle with fluctuating emotions as a result of hormonal changes, baby blues, or even the more extreme postpartum depression. If you experience intense, ongoing sadness, anger, or hopelessness, you should consult your doctor. But many new moms will experience degrees of these feelings as they transition into motherhood.

The apostle Paul offered this reminder, "Do nothing from rivalry or conceit, but in humility count others more significant than yourselves. Let each of you look not only to his own interests, but also to the interests of others" (Philippians 2:3–4, esv).

During the season of becoming a mom, which begins the moment you find out you're pregnant, it can be difficult to think of others (besides your baby, of course). You may feel exhausted and depleted, and you will have a lot of your own "interests" to think about. It's perfectly acceptable to be thinking about how you can best care for yourself and your baby.

But being a new mom isn't a free pass to lash out at others or disregard their feelings. Instead, make some room to consider the needs of others—your husband, family members, friends, and even the health professionals caring for you and the baby.

Failing to be flexible. Gracious behavior toward others requires humility and flexibility. I remember getting together with a friend

while we were both pregnant and feeling a little chastised by her ada-
mant opinions on cloth diapers, organic baby food, and intervention-
free childbirth. While I'm sure she didn't mean to make me feel bad for
holding different convictions (that in some cases centered more around
comfort and convenience than anything else), I felt judged.

Because of that experience, I tried to remember that those I inter-
acted with—including family members and friends—would not all
share my convictions (and that was okay!). Truth be told, some of *my
own* convictions changed once my baby was born (and morphed again
with baby number two).

Keep in mind that the way you treat your spouse, family members,
and friends during this season will set the stage for healthy relationships (and a robust support system) moving forward. Responding in a
Christlike way during stressful times requires that you stay spiritually
connected during pregnancy and during the first days and months of
your baby's life.

EXPECTANT FAITH

Author Catherine Claire Larson once wondered if she'd ever be a
mother. That's not to say that she didn't want to be one. "If you'd
asked me when I was a kid what I wanted to be when I grew up, a
mom and a wife would have been on the list," she says. "I thought that
would happen early in my life, but it didn't."

Instead, Catherine graduated from college and spent seven years
writing with Chuck Colson for *BreakPoint* radio as well as writing
columns for national publications.

Catherine continued to pray about being a wife and mother. "It
was always a desire and a hope and something I had to give to Jesus
and lay at His feet," she says.

God did provide her with a husband. They married when Catherine was thirty, and she became pregnant with their first child a year later. Today, Catherine has been married for five years and has three children. She has also written the book *Waiting in Wonder: Growing in Faith while You're Expecting*, a devotional and journal for pregnant women.

Though her path to motherhood was different than she expected, Catherine feels it uniquely prepared her to parent.

"You look at the people in the Bible who had to wait a long time," she says, "and God always did something special in their hearts. He prepared them in a very tender way through that waiting."

She even sees a benefit in being an "older" mom. "Even though older moms may be at a disadvantage physically—I feel my back aching a bit getting off the floor from reading stories—" she chuckles, "I think we may have an advantage in that our hearts have longed for motherhood, and we may treasure it in a deeper way because of that."

The extra time she had to cultivate her relationship with Christ during her single years has given her a passion for encouraging other women to draw near to Jesus during pregnancy.

"Raising children is such an important calling," she says. "You're taking on the responsibility not only of helping a little human develop into an adult, but also of helping him grow into the knowledge and understanding of who God is. That's a huge task. We can't do it on our own."

Catherine suggests that a mother use the season of pregnancy to fortify her own relationship with Christ in preparation for the challenges of motherhood.

"We need to prepare spiritually because motherhood is a season of intense sacrifice," she says. "It helps to understand the basics of what Jesus calls us to in discipleship—that He calls us to come and die. That He calls us to lay down our lives, and to pick up our cross and follow Him. As we prepare ourselves in this way, we are more ready to take on the sacrifices motherhood entails and to lay them down as offerings to Christ rather than the burdens this world would call them."

Building Your Faith

Catherine Claire Larson offers six ideas for moms to deepen their faith during pregnancy:

Read the Word. Pregnancy is a great time to draw closer to Jesus. That personal time gets scarcer with each child you have. Abide in Him. In the same way that baby is receiving sustenance in the womb through the umbilical cord, think about having your umbilical cord tied to Jesus and being dependent on Him for everything.

Seek out godly mentors. I sought out women in my church who I thought were a little bit ahead of me and from whom I could ask advice. We'd go out and get dessert and coffee. Find those women who are serious about following the Lord and being good moms. Pray for the Lord to provide those kindred spirits.

Pray for your baby. I've loved documenting prayers for my children. I hope they'll look back and see how much their mother loved them and how she prayed for them even when they were in the womb.

Journal. In the Old Testament God tells the Israelites to set up an "Ebenezer"—a monument—in remembrance of what He has done (see 1 Samuel 7:12). You can do that through journaling. Capture some of your feelings and emotions during this special season to look back on later. You can see what God was doing in your life and the seeds He was planting.

My mom handwrote the story of my birth in the back of my baby book. It's a treasure for me to read the story of how I came into the world, in the voice of my young mother. When our children are old enough to read the words we journal today, they are going to know us in a different way. It's a glimpse we can share with our kids of who we are and how we loved them.

Fall in love with Jesus. Pregnancy was one way I fell more deeply in love with Jesus—just seeing what He was doing through the creation of a new being inside of me.

Worship. Pregnancy is such a wondrous time as you think about the marvels of the baby's biological development. This time is such a window into worship as you think about how God knits this human being into life—how He brings something from nothing. Even the intricacies, such as the way the fingerprints form as the amniotic fluid swirls around the fingers, can inspire worship.

THE MYTH OF THE PERFECT MOM

Around the time I became pregnant, I got one of those apps on my phone that tracks the baby's development and tells you what you should be doing—or not doing—as a mom: "Drink more water," "Don't sleep on your back," "Do your daily 'kick counts.'"

Three years later, I still receive almost daily emails from the website that produces that app. And with each email, I can tend to feel a little more inferior. *Regular play dates are important for my child's social development? Oops. Have I looked into preschools? Uh, no. Organic foods only? Do chicken nuggets count?*

For better or for worse, moms these days are inundated with a wealth of information on the "best way" to take care of their children.

I recently read a blog post in which a mom mashed together all the conflicting "expert advice" on baby care, revealing that it was impossible to follow. The result was humorous because it was so true![1]

Commenting on the post, Linda Sharps in The Stir blog says: "I don't even know how people manage their *pregnancies* these days without going completely insane, what with the billions of confusing guidelines about what is and isn't okay—and it just gets crazier once you actually give birth."[2]

GREAT EXPECTATIONS

Chrystal Evans Hurst, author of *Kingdom Woman,*[3] which she co-wrote with her dad, Dr. Tony Evans, says new moms need to understand that caring for a baby will be challenging.

"One of the biggest things I hear new moms say is, 'I didn't know it would be this hard,'" Hurst says. "We live in a point in history where daily life has never been so easy. So the leap from caring mainly for yourself to having a child who is completely dependent on you can feel dramatic. It takes a lot of extra effort to have another person in your life who is dependent on you for everything."

In addition, Hurst explains, women often put unrealistic expectations on themselves. "We have these idealistic impressions of what we should be able to do as moms," says the mother of five. "The problem with Facebook and Pinterest and Twitter is that people only put their best foot forward. So you're thinking, *I should be the sum total of all the things I see.* And that's just not true—or possible."

Hurst believes the pressure of these expectations has contributed to the rise of postpartum depression and the overall stress of motherhood. "Not only are moms doing the job of every other mother through time, they're doing it with this extraordinary expectation that they don't need help. We have the mistaken impression that other moms are doing it all, and we're ashamed to say we're struggling. It's okay to need help. It's okay to *ask* for help. We can't do it all."

Later in this book, I will recount how I slowly slipped into a pit of isolation following the birth of my son. Some days I felt like I had traded in an exciting existence for life on a deserted island (otherwise known as our townhome), where I wasn't even that great at performing the mundane tasks expected of me. And because of the cute and impressive "mama highlights reel" I viewed on social media each day, I thought I was the only one.

PASSING BY PERFECTION

From the moment you hold that little bundle in your arms, you will likely feel pressure to be a perfect mom. And you will likely feel as if you're not living up to the task. And like Hurst pointed out, you may also feel like other moms are doing it better—a lot better.

Blogger Rebecca Stone recounts her experience of dealing with perfectionism. "The message I'd sent to myself over and over for most of my life was to try harder," she says. "Be more. Do and do and do. Be perfect. At everything."

While she was pregnant with her first daughter, Kyla, Stone felt overwhelming pressure to be the "perfect mom." She scoured Christian parenting books to find out what God expected of her. She writes on her blog:

> The tension built, as did the internal manual I was creating for myself. There were practically volumes by the time Kyla arrived. I was overwhelmed and overcome by the expectations, by my desire to be a good mom. I was also gripped with fear that I wouldn't do it right. In so very many different ways, I was sure I would mess this motherhood thing up, and I just couldn't

fail. I couldn't. For I believed that if I messed this up, if I wasn't perfect, that I was really disappointing God.[4] (Excerpted by permission.)

She says the story of Martha, "the ultimate perfectionist," in Luke 10:38–42, ministered to her. When Martha complained that her sister Mary wasn't helping with the tasks that needed doing, Jesus' reply was simple, Stone says:

He said this: "Only one thing is needed." What one thing? Listening. Sitting at His feet. You see, when we stop long enough to sit at His feet, we get to hear the Truth about who we are and what God has for us. When we are able to hear His voice saying our name, we find out that not all of the expectations we put on ourselves are the "better" thing. While some of them may be good, they are not the best.[5]

Instead of measuring themselves by impossible standards, moms need to focus on their calling. As moms draw near to God, He promises to draw near to them (see James 4:8). In the day in and day out tasks of caring for a baby, He is there.

I once heard a speaker at a women's retreat recount how, when she became a mom, she grieved the loss of the extended quiet times she used to have with the Lord. She no longer felt she had the time to indulge in the same rich moments with Him.

One day, as she went through the daily tasks of caring for her child, a verse from Matthew came to her mind: "For I was hungry and you gave me something to eat, I was thirsty and you gave me something to drink" (Matthew 25:35).

"As I extended that sippy cup of apple juice to my toddler," she said, "I heard Jesus say to me, 'Whatever you did for one of the least of these, you did for me.'"

In her blog post "Embrace the High Calling of Parenthood," Catherine Claire Larson writes:

> One day they will not remember the day at the water park or the long-saved-for vacation; they will remember how they felt when they were with me. Did they feel the daily drip of my despondency over my mundane role, or did they feel joy in my presence because I knew deep down my part mattered and their time under my care had eternal value?[6]

Being a mom matters. It is a sacred role that forever impacts the life of a child. Embrace the calling—not aiming for perfection but aiming for dependence on the One who has entrusted you with the task and equipped you for it. Some days that will look like an unimaginable number of diapers (and outfits) changed; other days it will look like the face of God.

TIME TO TALK

- What "kind of mom" do you think you are? Do you relate more to Becky or Julie from the beginning of this chapter?
- What are some of the expectations you have about your life as a mother? Using the list you created, discuss your expectations with your husband.
- Which of the "Momzilla" mistakes do you think you will be most prone to? (For instance, excluding Dad, failing to ask for help, expecting perfection, allowing yourself to behave badly.)

• What are two ways, provided in the list by Catherine Claire Larson, that you would like to incorporate now to strengthen your faith as you prepare to be a mom?
• Do you feel pressure to be a perfect mom? How can you give the burden over to the Lord?

Take some time to reflect on God's purpose and plan for you as a mother. Lay your desire for perfection at His feet and commit to dependence on Him as you take on this sacred role.

CHAPTER FOUR

Being a Dad

Now for the guys: Let's get real about impending fatherhood. When Greg Smalley attended the baby shower for his first child, he didn't expect to get schooled in fatherhood.

"We played this game that was a competition to see who could diaper a plastic baby doll the fastest," Greg says. "I played along and came in dead last . . . against grandmas, single women . . . I looked pathetic."

The failure motivated Greg to step up his dad skills. "I had this competitive streak going," he says. "I knew the fastest time, and I decided I was going to figure out how to do it faster!" To his wife's surprise and delight, he committed to changing every diaper when his daughter arrived.

Although he jokes about it now, Greg admits that the "great diaper defeat" shook his confidence. "I thought, *I lost. I came in last. I can't even change a diaper! How can I take care of a child?*"

These feelings lingered as he and Erin welcomed their daughter, Taylor. "I was afraid to hold her," he says. "I thought, *What if I drop her? What if I break her?*"

Greg got over his fears of fatherhood, but he points out that it was one of the first times he felt incompetent. "I had a certain level of confidence with who I was as a man and as a husband," he says. "When Erin got pregnant, it was confusing. I went from this secure, confident guy to not being sure what she needed. Her body was changing, and she had this unique bond with this little baby growing inside her that I didn't have."

Greg says rubbing his wife's belly and talking to the baby was "nothing compared to when that baby was finally in my arms. That's when the bonding really took place."

Baby-Daddy Bonding

As you're watching your wife's midsection grow, you may find it hard to grasp that your son or daughter is actually in there. And let's admit it, your wife has a certain advantage in bonding with the baby. That doesn't mean you can't find ways to connect right now.

Here are a few bonding ideas from other dads:

Daddy to bump. Dale says he talked to his wife's baby belly with both of his daughters and even played music. "I definitely think they both knew my voice right away," he says. "They would turn their heads when I spoke, as early as right after they were born."

Top student. Nick talked to his wife's baby bump and also went with her to all the prenatal appointments and classes. Although he didn't notice any specific recognition when his daughter was born, he says he felt more confident and prepared as a dad.

Do-it-yourself dad. To feel more connected with Baby-on-the-Way, Mike painted his daughter's room and refinished some baby furniture. "Spending time in the nursery acclimated me to the idea of having a baby around," he says. "And now that my daughter is older, she loves the idea that Daddy 'made' her room for her."

Picture it. At a prenatal visit Dan not only asked to hold the baby doll that represented the size of his twenty-week-old son—just to have a better feeling for the baby he couldn't yet see—he also took home the ultrasound picture and hung it in a prominent place. "I looked at the picture every day," he says, "and studied my son's features. I couldn't wait to meet him in person!"

Here are a few additional tricks that may help you feel close:

- Reading or singing to the baby in utero (babies can hear the outside world as early as sixteen weeks)
- Writing notes or emails to the baby
- Praying out loud for your son or daughter
- Accepting your wife's invitations to "feel the baby move"

FATHERHOOD: MISSION POSSIBLE

As you prepare to be a dad, you may be wondering about your role—now and once the baby arrives.

In the childbirth class Kevin and I attended before our son was born, the soon-to-be-dads expressed concerns about everything from supporting their wives during labor to providing financially for a baby's needs to bonding with their newborns. Preparing for the coming changes—physically and mentally—is one of the best things a new dad can do to get ready for life with an infant.

When asked how he prepared for being a dad, humorist, blogger, and best-selling author Jon Acuff responded, "Poorly. Is that an answer?"

Acuff says he eased his way into fatherhood, figuring it out as he went along. Having positive expectations helped. "I have parents who love me and are vocal in that," he says. "So I looked at having kids as a fun opportunity. I felt great about it. But I don't think I understood the boundless joy of coming home and having my kid run out the front door and into my arms. That's fantastic. That's hard to understand until you get there."

Realistic expectations are also a plus. Alan, the father of a toddler and newborn, says, "Be ready for the wave to hit. The loss of independence and spontaneity can be depressing. It's a beautiful season, but life certainly isn't about you anymore."

He also said he found connecting with a newborn awkward, but it became easier as the baby became more interactive. Every dad is different. Some will find it easy to connect with a newborn, while others may find greater enjoyment in parenting older children.

Acuff adds: "I don't think parents understand that when they're in the middle of first-time parenting, they're in a crisis. It's a beautiful crisis. It's a great crisis. But it's a crisis. You're all of a sudden *raising a human*! For the first few years, you don't understand that. Once your child is five or six, you look back and think, *No wonder it was hard for us to stay connected. We were in the middle of the tornado of a baby!*"

LONG LIVE THE COMPETENT DAD

I recently saw a commercial in which a dad ran around town doing errands with his infant son strapped to his chest in a baby carrier. This dad confidently, albeit somewhat chaotically, completes a number of domestic errands (we're to believe it's all thanks to a banking phone app) and then calls his wife to let her know everything's under control.

The reason I like this commercial is that it rings true to what I've observed in the dads I know. From the moment our son was born, Kevin has been a super-involved dad who never shied away from taking our baby to doctor's appointments, to the grocery store, or even to meet friends for dinner—by himself.

But for years, TV and movies have been depicting fathers as the opposite—incapable of caring for their children or handling simple household tasks. Or worse—unwilling. It's not only an insulting stereotype; it's untrue.

A LiveScience article gave this example of the backlash:

The bumbling dad stereotype is a favorite caricature for marketers. In March 2012, the diaper brand Huggies ran an ad campaign that called alone time with dad "the ultimate test" for their diapers—a phrasing taken to mean that fathers were too dumb to handle diaper changing. The brand quickly learned that modern dads don't take kindly to such implications. After an outcry and an online petition, Huggies pulled the ads and altered them to be more dad-friendly.[1]

Modern dads are much more hands-on with their kids than dads of the past. They are also highly capable of performing the responsibilities associated with caring for their children—and more willing, too.

According to the Pew Research Center, in 2011 fathers spent seven hours a week taking care of their children and ten hours doing housework (about half the hours put in by moms). That's way up from 1965, when dads provided only two and a half hours of childcare a week and did four hours of housework.[2]

Part of this shift has to do with moms working more hours outside the home (a topic that is covered more in depth in the next chapter). As Mom's hours away from the home and children increase, Dad's hours with the children, and his involvement in the household, increase.

Writer and blogger Joshua Rogers, who is also an attorney, sees the shift and says most of his friends who are dads are very involved with their children. "They know how to feed a child baby food, they help around the house, they play with their kids, and they can give Mom the night off."

Rogers, thirty-four, believes the cultural shift to a more competent and involved dad opens up new benefits for families. "Unlike previous generations, I think mine grew up with the expectation that we were going to be there for our families," he says, "which meant we were going to do more than bring home a paycheck—we were going to shoulder the burden of loving our families in the daily grind of life.

"And as we've done this, we've noticed that our kids are more connected to us, our wives feel less haggard and are more tender toward us, and our marriages and families are much happier. That makes life happier—everybody wins."

Researchers agree that children reap many benefits from having more quality time and interaction with their fathers. In one report on the significance of dads, sociologist Dr. David Popenoe notes, "Fathers are far more than just 'second adults' in the home. Involved fathers bring positive benefits to their children that no other person is as likely to bring."[3]

Dr. Popenoe draws a clear connection between involved fathers and positive outcomes in children, including cognitive ability, educational achievement, psychological well-being, and social behavior.[4]

Fathers are also critical to their child's spiritual development, including his or her understanding of God. In his essay "Incredible Privilege of Fatherhood," author Randy Alcorn explains this divine role:

Our fatherhood is the shadow; His [God's] is the substance,
which casts the shadow. As our marriages are to be signposts [of]
the marriage of Christ to His church (Ephesians 5), our father-

hood is to point our children to their Father in Heaven. We bear on our shoulders the reputation of our Father in Heaven. Whether they want to know Him and walk with Him will largely depend on whether they see Him or us.[5]

That's a pretty big calling. And it's one fathers need to take seriously. One concern dads in particular may have is how they will lead their family spiritually. Alex, the dad of six-month-old Owen, says, "The fact that I have more responsibility than ever is still sinking in. The time I spend with my son now is simple—blowing strawberries on his tummy, playing peek-a-boo, or reading him a book with more pages than words.

"But there will be a time in the near future where he begins to observe how I love Jesus and how I treat his mom. I've seen the tremendous pain that dads have brought into the lives of their children by not being a leader of their home. I know that, if I love the Lord first and foremost, He will give me the strength and wisdom to lead my family well."

Along with nurturing their personal relationship with God through Bible study and prayer, dads can seek out other men—both friends and mentors—who share and support their desire to raise godly children. In addition, they can plug into a church where they can receive support.

For two years, my husband, Kevin, has been meeting weekly with an older Christian man whose children are grown, and going through a curriculum that specifically looks at how to pass on faith to the next generation. Mentors are available through 4Gens, a ministry promoted by our church. "Being a reflection of Christ takes work," Kevin says. "Going through this curriculum is helping me know the foundations of my faith and who Christ is, so I'm prepared to live that out in front of my family."

FEARING CHANGE

When you think about being a dad, what do you picture? Take a few minutes to write down how you picture the following after you become a dad:

- My outward appearance _____

- My daily routine _____

- My relationship with my wife _____

- Our family finances _____

- My social life _____

- My ideal day _____

Identify the areas you think will change significantly and those areas where you expect to see little to no change. In which areas do you fear change the most?

Joshua Rogers says he had two main fears about how life might change once the baby arrived. The first, he believes, is a concern for most guys: *Will it ruin our sex life?*

"That fear turned out to be totally unfounded," he says, "but I think it was because we took practical steps to get romance back into our marriage after the baby was born." He and his wife chose not to have the baby sleep in their bedroom, he says, and they got a babysitter so they could go out on a date a few weeks after their daughter was born.

"I also made a point to remind my wife that she was still very beautiful to me," he says, "because I didn't want her feeling insecure about her postpartum body. As a result, we were sleeping better, we were emotionally connecting, and the next thing you know, well, she was pregnant again."

Along with his concerns about how he and his wife's relationship might change, Rogers was also worried he wouldn't get enough sleep and would be too tired to go to the gym each morning, something he'd made a priority for several years.

"I had to make adjustments to keep that part of my life intact," he says. "I used to get up to go to the gym at 6:00 AM. Now I get up at 5:05 because I like to get back home in time to see my kids when they wake up and help my wife get their day started."

Rogers admits it is a sacrifice. "Am I more tired than I would like to be sometimes? Yes, but I'm healthy, and my kids are able to start and end their day with Daddy, so it's worth it to me."

Jon Acuff on Work and Dreams

As an author and speaker, Jon Acuff meets many dads who are trying to strike a balance between pursuing their dreams and embracing the responsibilities of fatherhood. He offers these helpful tips:

On balancing career and family: Balance is a myth. I encourage folks to do the math. I had a friend who was an accountant; he only worked fifty hours a week (which is still a lot), while everybody else worked sixty hours. His supervisor said, "We're going to cut your bonus by $2,000 because you didn't work as hard."

My friend figured out that he got ten additional hours a week with his family, multiplied by fifty-two weeks. That's 520 hours. What if someone said, "I'll sell you 500 hours with your wife and kids for $2,000"? That's $4.00 an hour . . . to spend time with your family. That's a deal!

On having dreams: I meet so many guys who tell me, "I'm just not working on my dream hard enough. I could be hustling more. I'm being lazy."

I'll say, "Tell me about your family," and they'll respond, "Well, we have two twin four-month-olds and a three-year-old."

I tell them, "You're raising human beings. That's enough of a dream." I don't think we give parents the credit they deserve in our culture.

On dreaming responsibly: You have to be brutally realistic about your present circumstances and wildly unrealistic about your future circumstances. The problem with our culture is that it says be unrealistic about both. We are taught such a selfish definition of dreaming.

Any time I run into a dad who is like, "I have five kids, but I'm thinking about quitting work and going back to school and getting a master's in creative writing," I want to shake him and say, "You have responsibilities. This isn't dreamer time. You've got to be honest and realistic about the responsibilities you have to your family."

That doesn't mean you can't dream; it just means you have to dream in a responsible way.

My husband, Kevin, says he wasn't overly worried about the changes having a baby would bring. Our lifestyle already consisted of many quiet evenings spent at home—something that wouldn't change a lot with a baby (except perhaps the "quiet" part). And because we were still newlyweds, we also spent a majority of our time together. "I felt ready and eager to take on the responsibilities of being a dad,"

Kevin says. "Having children was something I had looked forward to and wanted since I was a teenager. I knew change was coming, but I was mentally preparing myself for it."

HAPPY WIFE, HAPPY LIFE

You've probably heard this saying before. And if you've been married for any length of time, you probably know there's a lot of truth to it. As we've already discussed, maintaining a healthy, happy marital relationship is key to the happiness and development of your child. But it's also primary to your happiness as a dad and your wife's happiness as a mom.

Here are a few ways to stay connected:

Be intentional. "You have to be deliberate about connecting with your wife," Acuff says. "We're deliberate about other areas of our lives, like work. You'd never trust that meetings at work would just happen, and you shouldn't think that way about date nights. You go to Outlook, you reserve a room, and you look at someone else's calendar—you're deliberate. Be deliberate about going out on dates. Do regular temperature checks on the relationship. You don't have to fight to drift apart." Find a babysitter through church or mutual friends. Plan a date where your wife doesn't have to handle all the details. Let her know that spending one-on-one time together is important to you.

Be attentive to her needs. Ian, a father of five, says sharing the load with his wife, Mindy, was a big part of his role when their first baby arrived. "I was Mindy's support," he says. "She knew what she was doing, and my role was to do whatever I could to help carry her burden. In those years, regular support was greater than date night."

Focus on teamwork. "Husbands want to be able to fix problems," Acuff says. "And babies come with problems that you don't fix—you hold the baby for an hour. My wife, Jenny, and I learned how to be a team. She always used to say, 'There aren't any magic fairies that live at this house. The stuff that happens, happens because I make it happen, and you need to make it happen too.'"

Change if you need to. A new baby can highlight areas of needed growth in a dad's life. Ian says having children fundamentally changed him for the better. "I was pretty selfish," he says. "I still am, but by God's grace, less so. Having kids aided my maturation. I'm afraid to think about where I'd be right now had that not been the case." For example, if you're one of those dads who loves to spend time playing video games, or you have a habit of being glued to your smartphone, realize that there's a time for that, and it's probably not while you have a newborn.

View from the Nursery
How to Forget Your Wife Is Wonderful[6]
by Joshua Rogers

"Make sure to record as many of your child's moments as you can, especially in the early years. You'd be surprised how quickly she will change."

I thought my co-worker's advice was good. So I decided to get a journal and—every day—write about one thing my daughter did and one thing my wife did. This little exercise in preserving our young family's history was going to teach me a lesson: I was forgetting to admire my wife.

My brief journal entries went something like this: "Today, I came into the room and found my daughter with a Tupperware container on her head. I got a good laugh out of that. My wife felt tired all day."

I also had a number of longer journal entries where I

wrote six or seven sentences about my daughter, gush-ing with detailed admiration about something adorable she did. Then I would remember to write about my wife and add something like, "My wife worked out today, even though she's six months pregnant. Go, Honey!"

It wasn't until a couple of weeks into my journal writ-ing that I saw the pattern: I would go on and on about my daughter and end by noting that—oh yeah, my wife is still alive. And even when I did write more colorfully about my wife, it was almost always about her role as a mother.

Then the thought occurred to me: "You know, my wife is someone's little girl, too. It's not like she stopped being cute and interesting just because we got married and had kids. And there's more to her than being a mom." So I started watching her again, looking for all those things that interested me when we first started dating.

It didn't take long before I realized that she frequently makes me laugh, she's a serious woman of prayer, she's very perceptive about people (especially me), and she still turns my head when she walks through the room. But I had taken these things for granted, and by the end of each day, the most beautiful things about her had passed me by.

As I started making a point to enjoy her as much as I enjoyed my daughter, my journal entries began changing. Rather than writing about a tired mom, I began writing about a gorgeous, godly woman who's fun to be around. And in a fresh way, with each journal entry, I realized all over again why marrying her was the best decision I ever made.

BALANCING WORK AND HOME

This goes along with the previous point about marital bliss. How you participate (or don't participate) in the home can have a major effect on your wife's happiness and the overall home environment.

Dr. Kevin Weary says he sometimes hears men say they can't help their wives around the house or spend time with the new baby because they "have to go to work."

He says, "I want to tell them, 'My job is pretty demanding, too. As an OB-GYN, I'm on call, and I work evenings. But I help my wife out around the house. I still spend time with her and my children.'"

Joshua Rogers adds, "As an attorney, I work in a field with a number of successful, ambitious, driven people. It's tempting to move with the current and stay at work late based on the 'I don't want to leave the office too early' guilt trip.

"I recently started a new job, and my (very unconventional) boss said something I won't forget: 'Joshua, you need to understand that everyone at this office is dispensable. If we die tomorrow, they'll replace us soon afterward, and everyone will move on with their lives. But there is one place in this world where you are never indispensable, and that is with your family. Always make them your first priority.'"

Matt McGee and his wife, Chantal, have been welcoming families to their Colorado ranch for marriage and family camps since 2004. He says he often meets fathers struggling to put their families first.

"There's a cost when dads don't show up," he says. He points to the example of King David found in 1 Chronicles 27:32. Buried in a record of who cared for the king's flocks, camels, and donkeys, is this verse: "Jehiel son of Hacmoni took care of the king's sons." McGee believes that David made a tragic mistake in outsourcing the care and instruction of his own children. Those sons went on to be rebellious, decadent, and unfruitful.

"David was focused on things outside his home far too often," McGee says, "and not only his immediate family but the nation of Israel suffered mightily because of that. If he had spent his time differently, I think history would have been different—not just for his family, but for the nation.

"I've heard many dads share through tears, 'I get home at the end of my workday, and I have nothing left to give to my spouse; I have nothing left to give to my kids. I expended the firstfruits of my energy and time outside the home.' And when that's really happening in a person's life, it *is* something to cry about. It is something that, if they don't change course, they will regret when this season is over—when they can't fix it anymore."

McGee suggests that dads think ahead to the end of their lives. *Who will I be most concerned about having impressed and made an investment in?* Most dads identify their wives and children as most important, after God. "I can work hard and as 'unto the Lord' at my job," McGee says. "But I have to remember that the most significant time of my day is when I get home."

FULL-TIME DADS

For some dads, taking care of the baby will be their primary job. With the rise of stay-at-home dads (discussed in the next chapter), more fathers are turning into career caretakers of their children than ever before. While it may be a little easier for these fathers to keep their focus on the home and family, this arrangement comes with its own unique challenges that dads will have to navigate to keep their families strong.

Abe, the father of two toddlers, stays home to care for his children. "When my wife, Grace, and I decided to have kids after eight years of marriage, she was working from a home office at a job she loved with great pay and amazing benefits," he explains. "We'd both been raised with stay-at-home moms and assumed we'd follow suit, but I was doing less-reliable contract work, so it made sense for me to become the primary caregiver."

Project Nursery

Decorating the nursery together can be a great bonding experience for couples as they prepare for their little one. Here are a few tips to help you get started:

Gather the furniture. Nursery furniture can be expensive, but if all new is out of your budget, you can find great deals at garage sales, online "buy and sell" sites for parents, or secondhand stores. Just be sure to be well versed on the latest safety standards for baby gear.

Personalize. Choose colors and a theme, and then consider details that will make the room friendly and functional, such as organizational bins and a rocking chair for nursing. Add a personal piece of artwork, a framed photograph, or a quilt created by you, a family member, or a friend.

Room to grow. Try to create a room your child can grow into. At first you may just be using the nursery for diaper changes and late-night feedings, but in a year or two, you may want a play area or a reading corner.

Do it together. So, one of you is big on home décor, and the other likes to build things? Perfect. Divvy up the tasks so you can each work on things you enjoy.

For the most part, Abe enjoys the flexible schedule and togetherness their situation provides. "We get to share special moments, like first steps," he says. "Grace can dash upstairs and be part of the experience."

A downside has been finding community. "Being a stay-at-home dad is lonely," he says. "There are lots of moms groups, but it's almost impossible to find dads groups." He's also faced some prejudice from others who wonder about his choice to be a stay-at-home dad instead of working a "real" job.

"At first, I felt pressured to add a second career label," he says. "But I've since learned to embrace my 'career.' Being a dad is as noble and God-ordained a career as any man could hope for. Always being there is an incredible gift to give your children."

And he realizes it's only for a season. "All too soon they won't need me anymore," he says, "and I can go back to my *real* job."

FAILING WELL

There are no perfect dads. But there are good dads. There are even exceptional dads. And the best dads foster a loving, honest relationship with their children. They also seek out ways to be better fathers.

This doesn't mean fathers can't ever fail. They can and they will. But then they can model what it looks like to repent and be restored. And sometimes, Randy Alcorn writes, you "may teach them more than you would have by never failing, and far more than pretending you don't fail."

Dr. Tedd Tripp, author of *Shepherding a Child's Heart*, recalls a time when he feels he "blew it" as a dad. When his children were teenagers, the whole family rode their bikes from their home in northeastern Pennsylvania to Niagara Falls.

"The ride was 650 miles round-trip," he recalls. "My plan was that when we got to the falls, we would take a whole roll of film—pictures of us with our bikes and Niagara Falls in the background."

In an era before digital cameras and the Internet, he planned to develop the photos and turn them into postcards he could send out to friends. But his son had another idea.

"About four pictures in, my seventeen-year-old son decided this was ridiculous. He started making faces, facing the other direction, and doing all kinds of things to ruin the pictures."

In a burst of anger, Dr. Tripp verbally laid into his son. "I lost it," he says. "I was cruel in what I said."

Dr. Tripp says the blowup hung over his family like a cloud until he told his son he was sorry and asked for his forgiveness. "I knew that I had behaved badly, and I was sorry," he says.

Years later, he was able to realize what motivated his angry outburst. "It was about pride. It was about the fact that I wanted to prove something to all of my friends. I wanted them to see the postcard and see us all there successful on our trip to Niagara Falls and think, *What a wonderful dad Tedd Tripp is!*"

Dr. Tripp says when dads are able to recognize the motivation behind their shortcomings—especially the ones that affect their kids—they can offer an example of heartfelt repentance to their children. "Getting to the heart is such a powerful thing," he says. "Today if I were in that situation, I could not only apologize for what I did, but I could say, 'I understand what was behind it—it was all about Daddy's pride and wanting to impress his friends. And that's so wrong and so ugly. Please forgive me.' That apology would have been much more meaningful."

Despite the fact that he didn't offer the perfect apology, Dr. Tripp's son forgave him, and they share a strong relationship today—

evidence that God blesses a father who humbly seeks to be the best dad he can be.

Even very young children are already watching to see if your behavior is consistent with what you say you believe. "Road rage" is something my husband, Kevin, admits to struggling with. And in the heat of the moment, he's prone to call out some choice words. One day as we were in the car with our two-year-old son, a driver merged too quickly into our lane, cutting us off.

"Avoiding more colorful terms, I artfully called the driver a 'ding-dong,'" Kevin said. The next thing he heard was a sweet little voice from the backseat calling, "Ding-dong. Ding-dong. Ding-dong."

"My son was only using a handful of words at the time," Kevin remembered. "It was in that moment I realized my sins are evident to my children, and they will make unwise choices based on my unwise choices. They say moms have eyes in the back of their heads, but kids have eyes *everywhere*. They're always watching you."

God has given you an incredible privilege, dads. He has appointed you to be the first—and most powerful—example to your children of their heavenly Father. Take on the challenge soberly—but with the knowledge that your Father is with you every step of the way.

TIME TO TALK

- On a scale of one to ten, how much confidence do you have in your ability to be a father?
- What are your expectations for what life as a dad will be like? Do you think your expectations are realistic?
- What are your biggest worries or concerns about how life will change after the baby arrives?

- In what ways do you plan to support and connect with your wife in this following season? Take a moment to tell your wife what it is you love about her—as a wife, as a person, as a mom-to-be.
- What do you think it will take to be an exceptional father?

Take some time to reflect on God's special plan for fathers in the lives of their children. Pray that through your successes and failures as a dad, God will enable you to reflect the heavenly Father in their lives.

CHAPTER FIVE

Planning Post-Baby Career Decisions

Some days I miss my job. My *old* job.

Caring for a baby and a toddler is definitely a job, but I miss getting ready for the day in relative leisure, dressing in a stylish outfit—cute shoes, matching earrings—listening to the radio on the way to work and answering emails from the quiet of my desk while sipping a latte.

When my son was born, I was thrilled to leave my job of ten years and take on my new role as a stay-at-home mom. Kevin and I decided that I would continue to do some writing and editing on the side to supplement our income and provide a creative outlet for me.

All the pictures I had in my mind of staying home with my baby and working as a freelancer were very glamorous. I imagined myself sitting at my desk, sipping coffee, and working uninterrupted as my infant son cooed from his bouncy seat. Then, when I'd accomplished a good amount, I'd dress him in one of his adorable little outfits, and we'd join my husband for lunch.

This is not what happened.

Oh, staying home with my son was a delight—particularly because I knew without a doubt it was what God had called me to. But it was harder than I expected, with more complications and frustrations than I could have anticipated.

I never imagined how much I would cling to my husband coming home promptly at 5:30 PM, like someone drowning clings to a piece of driftwood. Or how I would look like a hot mess for most, if not all, of the day, while I feverishly tried to complete more than fifteen minutes of work in one sitting, while also changing diapers, cleaning up messes, and planning dinners—all things I was not naturally gifted at doing.

After a few months of staying home with my son, I had to admit: I missed my job. I missed the adult conversation. I missed the rush of a deadline. I missed the sense of accomplishment and kudos I received for a job well done.

Still, I knew I was doing what God had called me to.

WOMEN AT WORK

Dads, don't let me lose you in this chapter. While at the moment we're talking about the somewhat controversial topic of moms staying home or going back to the office, these are decisions you make together as a couple. One of the biggest decisions an expectant couple will make is deciding on the working arrangements following the birth of a baby. According to the US Department of Labor[1], in 2012:

- 70.5 percent of mothers with children under age eighteen were either working or seeking work (68.3 percent of mothers with a spouse present and 75.2 percent of single moms).
- 64.8 percent of mothers with children under six years old were working.
- 57 percent of mothers with infants under a year were working.

These statistics encompass all mothers involved in the labor force, including those who work part-time, work from home, and are self-employed.

Research suggests that finances are the primary factor in a mother's decision to work. A study from the Pew Research Center reveals that up to 40 percent of American homes with children rely on the mother's income to meet financial obligations.

Responding to the study, one publication says: "Working mothers are so much the norm at this point that to even point that out seems unnecessary and incongruous."[2]

The reasons mothers work are numerous and varied. Some, who may prefer to stay home, have to work to pay off college debt or supplement a spouse's income. Others may be the primary breadwinner of the family or wish to continue in a particular career track. Still others say they feel happier and have more energy for their children when they work.

Jeff and Brandy had their first child five years into marriage. "We wanted to have a few years 'alone' before a baby joined the club," Brandy says. "We spent those years working, taking trips together, buying a home, and dreaming of the family we hoped God would bless us with."

When they learned Brandy was expecting, they were excited. "When we saw those two lines, we were beyond thrilled," Brandy says. But the prospect of a new addition also brought pressure—especially for Jeff.

"I kept thinking, *Now I'm responsible for another person!*" Jeff says. "I knew Brandy was capable of taking care of herself if she needed to, but when we found out the baby was coming, I realized there would be someone completely dependent on me for everything."

By that point, the couple had already had multiple conversations about whether or not Brandy would return to work after the baby. "Jeff wanted me to be able to stay home if I wanted to," Brandy says, "but he was supportive of me returning to work if that worked better for all of us."

The couple prayed about their decision. Then halfway through Brandy's pregnancy, she found out she would have the opportunity to go part-time once her daughter was born. Because she desired to keep working, but fewer hours, it was the perfect arrangement. And because Jeff held a flexible job, he was able to stay home with their daughter during the first few months while Brandy was at work.

The arrangement proved to be a plus for the couple. "I went in three mornings a week, and I loved it!" Brandy says. "Time with adults. Time to dress up. And Jeff got those mornings alone with our daughter, and he loved that."

MAN OF THE HOUSE

When I left my job to stay home with my son, Kevin and I were making about the same salary—me as an editor and him as a children's ministry director at a church. He half-jokingly offered to stay home with our son while I continued my career. (He claims that is still his "backup plan.") He explained that spending quality time with our son each day instead of going to the office held a certain appeal.

More than couples in the past, today's expectant parents have a legitimate choice to make about which parent—if either—will stay home with the baby.

According to the US Census Bureau, 32 percent of married fathers—approximately 7 million dads—care for their children under the age of fifteen for a significant part of each week. This figure is up from 26 percent in 2002.[3]

The economic downturn (beginning in December 2007 and ending in June 2009)[4]—in which more men than women lost their jobs—plays a big part in this trend. The woman is the breadwinner in 23 percent of American homes, according to the Pew Research Center.[5-6] This isn't surprising when you consider that women continue to excel in academic fields and continue to increase their earning power.

The *USA Today* article, "An American Role-Reversal: Women the New Breadwinners,"[7] published in March 2013, cites several reasons for the rise of the stay-at-home dad. Women are increasingly more educated than men—earning more bachelor's, master's, and doctoral degrees than their male counterparts. At the same time, men are still more likely than women to choose careers doing things with their hands, such as building or carpentry, which pay less and may not deliver steady work.

Women also fare better when it comes to health insurance—a must-have when it comes to raising a child. The article reports: "Professional women generally have this precious commodity. Blue-collar men often don't. When kids arrive, the couple's decision is often a matter of familial responsibility."

A final reason the article provides for the shift in cultural stereotype is that sometimes the man may truly have the better disposition for daily, long-term exposure to the kids.

This role reversal has freed moms who prefer to work and dads who like to nurture. "Patience"—when Dad has it naturally and Mom doesn't—is the attribute both men and women cite for flipping traditional roles.

Having Dad stay home isn't for every family. Because of cultural expectations, theological concerns, and other factors, the role of stay-at-home parent can prove to be more frustrating for a man than for a woman. But some couples find that the arrangement suits their family perfectly.

Real Advice for New Parents

What works best for another family might not work best for your family. Try out different bits of advice, and figure out your own family's best solutions.

—*Missy, mother of two*

Couples should discuss this option to see if it is something they feel will benefit their family. The good news is, today's families have expanded options for making ends meet and nurturing family life. Perhaps you believe a traditional setup is the way to go; if so, great! Or maybe you find that you're open to more outside-the-box possibilities; that's okay, too. The important thing is that you and your spouse seek the Lord together to discover His best plan for your family.

THE DAYCARE DILEMMA

Jessica remembers the first day she went back to work after having her son, Jeremiah. "It was my birthday," she says, "and he was three months old. When I dropped him off at the daycare center we had found for him, he had a dirty diaper and was screaming.

"I tried to explain to the girls working there that he needed to be changed. I sat him down on the floor and put his car seat in the other room. When I came back, he was still on the floor, screaming. I went to the car and bawled. Then I called my husband, Jim, and said that we could *not* do this to our baby."

Jessica faced every mommy's worst return-to-work nightmare that day. She admits that she didn't put a lot of thought into her decision to go back to work. "I went back because it was what I knew," she says. After her unnerving daycare experience, she found a woman through a moms group at church who was willing to watch Jeremiah along with her own three daughters.

When Jessica gave birth to a second son, Josiah, two years later, she and her husband felt the timing was right for her to stay home. But she got more than she bargained for. "Staying home with the boys was a huge challenge for me," she says. "I've never been the artsy-craftsyhome-cookin'-clothes-making supermom like my mom when I was growing up."

With a demanding infant and a busy toddler in need of stimulating activities, Jessica says she felt frustrated and missed working. "Jim actually told me that he thought I had more energy for the boys when I was working," she says, "because I would focus on them when I was with them."

When a new job opportunity came up, Jessica returned to work, arranging a babysitting-daycare combo for her children's care. "We prayed about it and tried to discern the best thing for the boys," she says, "and this was it."

WHEN HOME IS WHERE YOUR HEART IS

Denise says her views on being a working mom were formed, in part, by her own mother, who stayed home from the time Denise was very young.

(It is interesting to note that one's own situation growing up can play a big part in one's expectations on this topic. Men and women who had stay-at-home moms are more likely to assume their family will be the same. Likewise, individuals who had working moms may see it as completely normal and reasonable for the mom to return to work.)

Denise always assumed she'd be a stay-at-home mom like her own mother. She even chose a career in public relations—a job she knew she could freelance—with her future goal of being a wife and mother in mind. Then came grad school. "It was a tough choice," she says. "I really wanted to do it. I'm a super nerd—I love school. But I didn't want to incur the debt." Still, with no boyfriend on the horizon, "I figured marriage wasn't a guarantee, so I took the plunge."

Denise also hoped the degree would help her excel to a place in her career field where she would be allowed flexibility if she became a wife and mom in the future. "I gave it my all during the early days of my career," she says. "I worked insane hours, honing my craft and working hard to be *good*."

Five years ago, when Denise married her husband, Andrew, he had been working at a profitable home contractor business in a different state. "We bought a fixer-upper that was in almost uninhabitable condition, so it was a full-time job for him to fix it," she says. Each day, Denise went to her job at a large nonprofit organization, and Andrew stayed home and fixed the house. "That was fine because we were childless."

When the couple did become pregnant, Denise was able to work out a flexible schedule with her workplace.

"My daughter rocked my world," she says. "I was completely enthralled by her and dreaded going back to work. My job and career, which had previously consumed such a huge part of me, suddenly didn't matter when I compared it to my baby. No one can explain the overwhelming love a mom has for her child; it's something you have to experience to understand."

Though she longed to stay home with her baby, doing so just wasn't an option: "I was the one with a steady job and health benefits."

Denise shed tears on her first day back, but she tried to settle into the "new normal." Then, when her daughter was three months old, she unexpectedly became pregnant with her son.

Denise and Andrew worked out an arrangement where the kids would always be at home with at least one parent. Andrew continues to take contracting jobs as he can and watch the kids when Denise is at the office.

View from the Nursery
Embracing My Version of Motherhood
by Rebecca Stone

I was barely a wife before I became a mom.

About six weeks after my husband and I got married, we found out we were pregnant with our first daughter. My husband was still in undergrad at the time, with plans to get a master's degree in counseling.

Kyla was born in November that year, and we celebrated our first anniversary in December. I worked full-time until the sixth month of my pregnancy and did my best to ward off all the unwanted mothering advice I received in our little town (where the church my husband worked for was literally in a cornfield).

When we moved to my home state of Colorado a short time later and Jeff started graduate school, I found myself doing something I never expected: I became a working mom.

In order for my husband to follow his calling to earn a counseling degree and go to seminary, I had to become the breadwinner.

In many ways, I had been reeling since the moment I found out I was going to be a mom. I had wanted time to prepare for motherhood. I didn't ever get that, and nearly every morning for seven years when I got ready for work, I felt like a failure.

The message I received while growing up was that working mothers are selfish and don't love their children as much as moms who stay home. In spite of feeling the pressure of an unrealistic checklist, I loved Kyla (and since then her sister,

Kaelyn) deeply and believed in my husband's calling.

Because I haven't lived up to my own expectations for motherhood, I've wasted too many breaths trying to convince others and myself that I'm a "good mom." At times, I've blamed God or my husband for our position in life, even though, deep down, I knew that wasn't the reason I felt so awful every morning.

Then, one day, I had an epiphany.

I started asking myself some questions: "What if I stopped worrying about all the things I wasn't doing on a daily basis and instead parented out of what I was doing—the things I love, my own experiences, and what God is doing in me? What if, because of working, I now have a set of skills I would never have had before? And, what if I was now able to pass those skills along to my girls? Skills such as conflict resolution, communication with a team, and creativity under pressure."

From that place, I started embracing motherhood with confidence. I acknowledged who God made me to be. I am a writer. I am a communicator. I am called to support my husband's calling and be a leader in God's church.

My girls are cared for, and my story is different from every other mom's. Some moms homeschool. Some practice law. Some love doing daily art projects with their children. Other moms write books and speak at conferences.

There is room for all of us, and we need to come alongside each other. We are not only our roles: wife, mother, employee, stay-at-home parent. We are the fullness of who God made us to be. That's what I hope to show my girls, through my actions and my words.

"I went into motherhood thinking that being a stay-at-home mom is a better thing for the family, so I've wrestled with mommy guilt," she says. "I'm not the mom I'd like to be. I can't cook the meals I'd like and keep the house as clean as I'd like. It's forced me to depend on God more—the kids won't turn out well solely because of me, but because of Him."

Denise feels one major positive of her family's arrangement is the teamwork style of parenting she and Andrew have developed. "There is an intense sense of partnership that I don't think we would have without struggling our way to it," she says. "Andrew is a much more hands-on dad than he would've been otherwise. The kids benefit from that."

MAKING THE DECISION

Deciding as a couple what your work and childcare situation will look like once your baby arrives is an important and personal decision. Here are a few things to consider:

Pray for direction. Author Catherine Claire Larson suggests that couples be intentional about seeking the Lord as they make the decision whether the woman will work outside the home or be a stay-at-home mom.

"A woman needs to seek the face of Jesus and listen to what He has for her, as well as talk to godly people who know her," Larson says. "No one can tell you what Jesus is telling you."

Larson left a prestigious job writing for *BreakPoint* radio to be a stay-at-home mom. "That was really hard," she says. "I thrived in that place. But I realized the time is short; in the grand scheme of things, the time you have with your children while they're little is very brief."

Know your priorities. When Denise had to go to work outside the home due to financial reasons, she and her husband, Andrew, made a list of their priorities as a family.

"There are certain realities we just have to deal with, such as the economy," she says. "But we asked ourselves, 'What are the things we know the children need?' Stability, love, security. There are different ways you can provide that and still be a God-honoring parent.

"Both Andrew and I have made sacrifices so that our kids always have one of us taking care of them. We've had to think creatively about how we can accomplish goals we have for our family. It takes a lot of work and a lot of talking things through, but it's possible."

Think creatively. When Jessica qualified for a job in government foreign service, she and her husband, Mike, had to figure out childcare for their infant daughter, Eva.

During the couple's first international assignment to South America, Jessica says, "I went to work, and Mike stayed home for the first year. After a year, he found a job at the embassy and went to work as well. We entered Eva in an excellent half-day preschool, where she really thrived. In the afternoons she was at home with a nanny."

Back in the States now—with the recent arrival of a second daughter—and awaiting their next international assignment, Jessica says she and Mike are happy with the arrangement. "We are blessed with a shorter, more flexible schedule now that will allow one of us to leave the house at 9:00 AM and another to be home by 3:00 PM each day, so we get to spend plenty of time with our daughters."

Jessica says she and Mike are still evaluating what they'll do when they go to North Africa next year. "Mike may work, or he may stay home again." Jessica points out that it is difficult for the spouses of US foreign workers to form social connections without an outlet in that country, such as a job.

"I never set out to be a full-time working parent," she says, "but we both felt that this opportunity was a calling for me to pursue, and that has been confirmed over our four years in government service. I love my career, and we are both happy with the lifestyle."

Leave your options open. In her article "The Accidental House-wife," Kimberly Eddy, who confidently assured her boss that she would be back to work six weeks after her daughter's birth, writes:

> It had been four weeks since I had given birth to my daughter, and I was struggling to figure out just how I was supposed to hand someone my precious baby and spend my first day back at work without her. I hated to admit it, but . . . somehow giving birth did change the way I felt about having children, motherhood, and my career.[8]

Like Eddy, a significant number of women who have worked full-time find that their values and desires change dramatically when their babies are born. Dr. Juli Slattery adds, "You can have it all written out when you're six months pregnant, and when the baby comes, you may have a completely different attitude. Leave room for God to work."

Think through several different arrangements you and your spouse could pursue after your baby arrives. Perhaps a restructuring of your budget would allow you to live on less and give up one income. Maybe one of you can bring in supplemental income through freelance work or a home-based industry. Or it may be possible for one or both of you to work a more flexible schedule.

When Wes and Nica learned they were expecting their first child, they realized the career they'd had the past eight years—traveling around the US with a comedy improv troupe—wouldn't be practical for this new season of life.

"Since our dating days, it had been important to us both that Nica would have the ability to stay home with our children," Wes says. "We naturally decided that riding around in a van with a couple of other dudes was no longer a viable career path . . . for either of us."

The couple transitioned into operating their own freelance video and film production company. "It felt like God was constantly giving us the next step exactly when we needed it," Wes says. "My wife has always been an integral part of our business, managing our motion graphics and art department. But it's always when and if she can. The kids take first priority. When we have to hire people, that's money our family loses, but it's time that our family gains. It's worth it."

LEAN UP

Dr. Juli Slattery says she recently read *Lean In,* a book by Sheryl Sandberg, the chief operating officer of Facebook. In it, the author encourages women to put their careers first in order to reach their full potential.[9]

"Her advice is don't let kids get in the way of your career path," Dr. Slattery says. "When I was reading the book, I kept thinking, *lean up.* Instead of looking to *my* goals and mile markers, I want to lean into God and ask Him, 'What do You have for me to do in this season?'"

Dr. Slattery says her own career goals did not go as planned. She earned her doctorate in psychology the same week she gave birth to their first son. "After years of schooling, I was working two nights a week, and my husband was the breadwinner," Slattery says. "I felt like I was giving up all of my career dreams. But I look at all the doors God has opened for me in His time, and I know I couldn't have planned it like that. If you trust God, hold your plans loosely, and are faithful with what He gives you, He blesses that."

When Kevin and I found out we were expecting, we already knew I would stay home with our son. We both came into marriage with that hope, and we prayed and strategized about how we could make it happen. "In this day and age, it can be a much more difficult decision to make," Kevin says, "because most of us are driven, in part, by the American Dream—wanting the nice house, the nice car, the nice vacations. You may have to make sacrifices and be intentional about what you want for your family.

"For us, that intentionality meant me seeking out a better-paying job so my wife would not need to return to work. It also meant downsizing our 'fun' budget for things like travel and eating out. Taking some steps to improve our financial situation allowed us to make our decision based solely on where we felt God was calling us as a family."

Denise adds, "I think sometimes we get caught up in the trappings of our culture and what our situation *should be*." Instead of worrying about an imperfect situation, she says, look for the ways God is providing for His particular plan for your family.

Though her own situation hasn't worked out in exactly the way she'd hoped, Denise sees God's hand in it. "It's caused us to sacrifice financially and professionally," she says. "It's caused us to be humbled. It's caused us to work hard. It's caused us to have many conversations about what's best for the kids and for our marriage. It's caused us to be intentional. It's caused us to depend on God. All of these things are good things."

TIME TO TALK

- Discuss what both of your expectations are for the work situation following the arrival of your baby. Are these based on your family of origin, cultural norms, or something else?
- What options do you have for work and childcare following your baby's birth? Is there anything you can do now to give yourself more options?
- What are your "big picture" priorities for your child, family, and home? (For example: love, security, consistency, etc.)
- How can you accomplish those goals with the work situation you will have?

• Setting aside the immediate work situation, what do you envision five years from now? How will you get there?

Pray as a couple for God to reveal His will to you on work matters. Ask for His provision and the ability to carry out your big-picture priorities in whatever situation you find yourself.

CHAPTER SIX

Surviving the Social Side of Pregnancy

We've established that as soon as you're pregnant, plenty of people want to share their negative stories with you, as was the case for Kevin and me. That's why at some point early on in my pregnancy, Kevin and I agreed not to listen to the naysayers.

We decided that since everyone's experience is different, *our* experience might be more pleasant than the cup-half-empty types had described. And, wouldn't you know it, it was. As we welcomed our son, I saw the best come out in my husband as he stepped up his game to help me care for our baby. And our first week as a family wasn't overly challenging as people had warned, but warm and memorable, culminating with Christmas Day.

That doesn't mean that there weren't adjustments along the way. I remember a minor incident from the first week that demonstrated this. A few days after we arrived home from the hospital, Kevin and I were discussing how my brother-in-law would drive him to the mechanic for a car issue the next morning. It was a simple errand that just a week earlier I would have done. Now I felt like I couldn't. I burst into tears—over driving to the mechanic!

When I explained how I felt, Kevin said, "You can drive me. We can put Josiah in his car seat, and you can go! This thing is what we make it."

Though I let my brother-in-law complete the errand, my husband's words were comforting. Things were going to change with a baby; I knew that. But we didn't have to be restricted by other people's experiences. How we moved forward as a couple and family would be up to us. And the same can be true for you!

LOSS OF PERSONAL SPACE

I'm convinced that whoever coined the proverb, "It takes a village to raise a child," was intending from in utero. At least it seems that when "the village" learns a woman is pregnant, they immediately clamor to join in on the raising. When we announced our happy news, we quickly learned that people will give you advice (lots of advice). Some you might disregard; some you might take to heart. It's your choice.

My wake-up call came when I was eighteen weeks pregnant—just beginning to show—and the twenty-something male cashier at my local grocery store remarked on my selections with a goofy grin, "Cravings, huh?" No matter that nothing in my meager grocery order was remotely out of the ordinary, he had an uncontrollable desire to acknowledge that I was "with child." I am not the only pregnant woman to receive this kind of oddly familiar treatment. Here are a few other awkward pregnancy stories:

> When I was eight months pregnant, my husband and I went to a concert. I walked into the bathroom, and this woman I didn't know jokingly said (*really* loudly), "Well, we know what *you've* been doing!"
> —Ashleigh

> At a gas station, a twenty-something guy shouted across the parking lot, "Whoa! You are huge! When are you due?" When

I told him, "Any day now," he proceeded to point me out to his brother.

—Johanna

A lady at work, who I barely knew, came over, squatted down to my belly, and began speaking baby talk to it!

—Amy

"Even strangers do weird things to pregnant women," says OB-GYN Kevin Weary. "They come up and touch them. And they think it's an invitation for personal conversations. It's okay to find a way to say no and divert those conversations."

Dr. Weary remembers a situation from his own wife's pregnancy where a woman approached them in the mall and said, "Ooh, can I rub your belly? It's good karma!"

"I wanted to say, 'No, that's called assault!'" he says, laughing.

And, in fact, Pennsylvania recently outlawed touching a pregnant woman's belly without asking permission. It may sound like one of those wacky, outdated state laws—such as it's illegal to wear a false mustache in church (Alabama) or wash your dentures in a public drinking fountain (Kansas)—but obviously it's needed![1]

If we're totally honest, for whatever reason, being pregnant seems to inspire the curiosity and participation of others. At some point during your pregnancy, you will very likely face some awkward moments and unsolicited advice.

Though these interactions can be a little (or a lot) annoying, the positive side is that pregnancy is a season when others are naturally drawn to you. And believe it or not, their openness to talk on a more personal level can instigate some good conversations that lead to opportunities to share Christ.

During my pregnancy, Kevin and I were able to befriend our

neighbors, who were due to have a baby around the same time, and even invite them to church. That connection may have never formed had they not noticed my pregnant belly. Stay focused on the positive. My friend Amber shared with me, "It's really fun looking obviously pregnant (rather than just wide). I've had a couple of older mamas and grandmas *ooh* and *aah* over my bump and give the sweetest advice and encouragement. I'm thankful for these moments!"

THE GRANDPARENTS

Lydia Harris, author of *Preparing My Heart for Grandparenting*[2] and grandmother of five, remembers the day she heard the news that she was going to be a grandma. "Our daughter and her husband invited us to meet them for dinner at a restaurant," she says. "As we finished the meal, our daughter handed us a gift. Inside we found a photo frame inscribed with, 'I love Grandpa and Grandma.'"

Harris says she and her husband were delighted by the unexpected announcement proclaiming their newest title as grandparents. "We appreciated knowing months beforehand about upcoming births so we could look forward to them," she says. "It also gave us time to clear our calendar to help out if needed and spend time with our newborn grandchildren."

Erin Smalley points out that finding special ways to include your baby's grandparents in the pregnancy and birth can contribute to healthy relationships later on.

"You're laying the groundwork and patterns that will be continuing throughout the years," she says. "This is a time to honor and love. Your children are going to treat you the way they've seen you treat your parents."

Harris adds that it's helpful to remember that the birth of your baby is a momentous event for your parents. "When a child is born, a grandparent is also born," she says. "When my husband and I stepped into the room to meet our first grandchild, we stepped into a new stage of life. Proverbs 17:6 says, 'Children's children are a crown to the aged.' From God's viewpoint, a coronation took place at our grandson's birth. We were crowned grandparents!"

The benefits of fostering good relationships with your child's grandparents are many, including childcare (if they live close by), a seasoned perspective, and even, in some cases, the spiritual training a grandparent can provide.

Awesome Announcements

Finding a cute way to announce your pregnancy to "the grandparents" is a great way to include them in their grandchild's life from the beginning.

- Find an item such as a bib or picture frame that uses "Grandpa and Grandma," and give it as a gift.
- Find or make a card announcing the news. (One couple made the announcement around Mother's Day by adding a handwritten "and Grandma" after the words "You're a great mom" inside the card.)
- Send them an e-vite to the "birth" (due date).
- Mail them a pair of baby socks or a pacifier with a handwritten note.
- Wear articles of clothing, or pins, that announce you will soon be "the mom" and "the dad."

Donna, an RN and grandmother of eight, says, "Grandchildren who develop relationships with grandparents have people besides their parents to encourage and rejoice with them over their childhood accomplishments. Grandparents add new perspectives and can sometimes provide experiences that parents cannot. Grandchildren have a place to go other than home where they are loved, accepted, safe, and can have fun. Sometimes they can share their problems with grandparents. They learn to value older people and the relationships they build with them. All this carries over into life as a strengthening force."

Unfortunately, dealing with family does not always go smoothly. Pregnancy can be a stressful season, and relationships with extended family can intensify. Consider how you might respond to these real-life scenarios:

- Your mother-in-law is a midwife and wishes to attend the birth.
- Your wife's mother has offered to come and stay for a month once the baby is born.
- Your husband has a large extended family that insists on visiting you in the hospital, one by one, and holding the baby.
- Your mother-in-law offers lots of unsolicited and critical baby-care advice.

Min says that in her Korean culture, mothers-in-law have a bad reputation for being pushy and overbearing, so she was prepared for the worst. After the birth of Min's first son, her mother-in-law, a longtime neonatal intensive care unit (NICU) nurse, came to the hospital for a visit.

"She came into the room, watched me breast-feeding, and told me I was doing it wrong," Min says. Without warning, she then gave an up-close and *physical* demonstration of how to better squeeze out the milk. "She was used to this because she helps new mothers in the hospital," Min says, "but I was not!"

Min recovered from the embarrassing moment, and her mother-in-law continues to be a regular part of her children's lives. "I spend a lot of time listening to what she has to say. I may not agree with it or always want to hear it, but I try to be a listening ear."

Justine has also dealt with outspoken in-laws. "My in-laws don't mean to come across as critical," she says, "but they also don't worry about hurting someone's feelings if they think changes need to be made." One day, shortly after Justine's daughter was born, her husband's family gathered at his grandmother's house. "My daughter started crying because she was hungry, so I asked for her so I could feed her. My mother-in-law rolled her eyes and said the baby was just 'exercising her lungs.' Then she said, 'Well, if that's how you want to mother.'

"I had to excuse myself to go to the bathroom—not because I needed to use it, but so I could have privacy to cry and pray for patience and strength."

Erin Smalley notes that when family stresses arise, grace is paramount. "Remember that it's such a gift to have the support and excitement of others," she says. "And their intentions are typically good."

She suggests that if you have a negative encounter with an in-law or parent, think of three to five positive things about the person to balance your feelings. "Often they're just trying to help," she says.

Real Advice for New Parents

Your mother-in-law, friends, and nosy strangers may be full of advice on what you should be doing as a parent, but in the end, no one knows your baby better than you do. Find out what works for your family and your baby in the current phase, and be flexible to adjust your approach for the next phase.

—Grace, mother of two

At the same time, mothers and fathers should remember that they have the ultimate say in their child's life. "It's okay for you to want something different," she says. "Your opinion and conviction might be different than theirs. Be honoring and kind, but remember that *you're* the parent."

Dr. Greg Smalley adds, "As a couple, you may still be trying to figure out how to separate from your families and be your own family unit. Know that you're the decision maker. You don't need to get into power struggles."

At the same time, he says, "See if you can accommodate what others need and want. Sometimes when our parents ask us to do things that might not be our first preference, we think, *It's not going to kill us to serve them.*"

THE OTHER MOTHER

Speaking specifically about mothers-in-law, I've been blessed and thankful to have a good relationship with mine. (In fact, I wouldn't be able to write this book without the free childcare she provides.) That doesn't mean we always think or do things the same way. This truth became evident shortly after I married Kevin. One day, as I folded my husband's undershirts, I discovered his last name professionally printed inside the collars.

When I asked him about this curious feature, he told me his mom had ordered them this way from the company (who knew you could?) so they would not get mixed up with anyone else's or lost. My mother-in-law's attention to detail was evident in this feature—and in her excellent housekeeping and organizational abilities.

I don't excel in the same areas. And without grace and goodwill, I might become frustrated in my inability to compete. Instead, I try to focus on the way God has gifted us differently and the significant ways in which my mother-in-law has contributed to my husband's life as well as our family's.

I realize that not every mother-in-law/daughter-in-law relationship is ideal. I've heard the horror stories of competition, clashing of wills, and uncut apron strings. And the truth is, some family relationships are just always going to be challenging. In tense moments, I've found it helpful to remember that just as God loves me and accepts me as part of His family, I am called to love my family—and that includes my husband's family.

Perhaps you are approaching the birth of your baby with an already-strained relationship with your mother-in-law (or another family member). In her blog post "How to Live with, and Love, Your Mother-in-Law," Erin Davis writes:[3]

> The mother-in-law/daughter-in-law relationship seems to really get slippery when the next generation arrives. Suggestions about how to burp and diaper a new baby can turn into fighting words.

As encouragement, she points to the story of Ruth, who includes her mother-in-law, Naomi, in the celebration of her son's birth. Davis writes: "Daughters-in-law, realize that your baby reminds your mother-in-law of her own babies and that she desperately wants to be a part of the celebration."

HANDLE WITH CARE

As you get closer to welcoming your little one, anticipate that family members will want to be involved, and decide on the best ways to include them.

Greg Smalley emphasizes that there are times to set boundaries with loved ones—for their benefit and your own. "A boundary is put in place to keep your heart open to the other person," he says. "If you get hurt and frustrated, your heart shuts down. So when you're setting a limit with someone, you're doing it to better love them, not to prohibit love."

He suggests that couples discuss the details of how family will be involved on delivery day and the days that follow. "Talk to each other about your expectations and the realities of family dynamics," he says. Some specific topics he recommends that couples discuss are:

- Who will we allow in the delivery room?
- Who will be welcome in the recovery room and at what times?
- If more than one set of grandparents is present, who will get to hold the baby first?
- Will we allow guests to stay at our home during the first few weeks? If so, who and for how long?

"Bring your desires and expectations out in the open," he says, "but plan to be flexible."

Even though my sister was in town from another state when I delivered my son, my husband and I decided we only wanted the two of us and our doula in the delivery room during labor. But as my labor intensified and other family members relocated to the waiting room, I realized that my sister was filling a crucial role, bringing me water, speaking encouraging words, text-messaging my family, and helping Kevin make me comfortable. I asked her to stay, and her help was invaluable.

Another decision Kevin and I had to make was whether we wanted our first few weeks to be "just us" or to include visits from my out-of-state family. (His family lives nearby, and we would usually be together anyway.) Because Josiah would be sleeping in a bassinet in our room, we chose to leave a bed in the nursery (that had formerly been our guest room), so we could welcome overnight guests. Because Josiah was born a week before Christmas, Kevin and I decided that it would be a good time to have visitors while my parents and others had time off work.

YOUR INNER CIRCLE

As you prepare to welcome your little one, you can expect social dynamics to intensify with strangers, friends, and family. But be on the lookout for something else. Look for those people who are rooting for you and can be part of your support system.

"Surround yourself with those who will speak life and encouragement to you," Greg says. "Hebrews 3:13 says we should encourage one another daily. There are only two places in the Bible where it says to do something every day: Take up your cross daily, and encourage one another daily. We need to be intentional to identify those who will encourage us."

As you prepare to welcome your little one, take advantage of opportunities to build new relationships and strengthen existing ones. Cultivating healthy, strong relationships with "the others" who love your baby opens up long-lasting benefits for everyone.

Real Advice for New Parents

Blogger and father of twins Matt Walsh puts it this way: "The problem is that anyone can easily describe the stressful things; the good things, on the other hand, are much more difficult to illustrate. Difficult only because they're so deep and transcendent and immeasurable. I can tell you about the love, and the joy, and the beauty, but even those words fail to contain how I feel about my children."[4]

TIME TO TALK

- What awkward situations, advice, or horror stories have you encountered? How did you respond? (You may want to write these down, as they will likely be funny later!)
- Make a list of the things you are looking forward to about being a parent. Hang this list on your bathroom mirror or the refrigerator, where you can look at it each day.
- What are some ways you can include your baby's grandparents in this special season?
- What expectations do you and your spouse have about how your families will be involved in the birth and the first few weeks?
- Do you have any concerns about how family relationships might be stretched or strained with the coming events? How can you "love and honor" your family while also setting appropriate boundaries?

Ask God to use your pregnancy to bless those around you and strengthen your relationships with your families.

CHAPTER SEVEN

Emotions and Pregnancy Fears

A few years ago, I remember hearing this quote about parenthood:

> Making the decision to have a child is momentous. It is to decide forever to have your heart go walking around outside your body.
> —Elizabeth Stone

As true as the sentiment is, the baby doesn't have to be on the outside for you to start feeling that terrifying, helpless love for your child.

For me, the feeling began when Kevin and I went to those early doctor's appointments. The first few times we got to hear our baby's heartbeat, I held my breath until the doctor was able to locate the right spot and we heard the gentle swish, swish.

In the days before I could feel the baby move, I wondered about that tiny person each day, hoping that he or she was alive and well. At ultrasounds, I hung on the technician's every word and facial expression, trying to discern even a hint of alarm. If she returned to look at the heart again, I wondered if something was wrong. And on those days when the baby's kicks weren't as noticeable, *I noticed*. I drank orange juice, lay on my side, and prayed until I felt that bouncy sensation in my middle.

Being parted from that little one was one of the worst things I could imagine—a fear that had previously been nonexistent.

DOCTOR'S APPOINTMENTS

You have probably been receiving prenatal care since you were around eight weeks pregnant. Most women choose their doctor during the first trimester and have between ten and fifteen prenatal visits. It can feel a little odd to go to the doctor so often if you have previously been healthy. And depending on your experiences with doctors and hospitals, these visits may even cause some anxiety.

Dad may or may not attend all these appointments, depending on schedules and availability. That's okay. Even if you're on your own, these appointments are a great time to ask questions, state your concerns, learn more about the labor and delivery process, and build trust and rapport with your physician.

During this time, even small discoveries about your baby can feel like a big deal. Joshua, the father of two, says he remembers one such occurrence during a prenatal appointment with their first baby. His wife's doctor told them they were having a boy, and then four weeks later announced that they were having a girl.

"You would not believe how much tension that created," Joshua says. "We played it cool in the doctor's office, but when we got in the car, my wife and I started arguing. We wanted to blame someone for the fact that we let ourselves have expectations about a gender that wasn't accurate. It took us about three days to recalibrate our vision of parenthood."

At our first ultrasound, Kevin and I learned that our son had an abnormality with his umbilical cord that could potentially interfere with his growth. In many cases, though, the abnormality did not pose a threat to the baby's health. Our doctor emphasized that he was not worried, and we didn't need to be either. At his suggestion, we avoided Google and enjoyed the additional ultrasounds we received.

PREGNANCY LOSS

One of the biggest fears a couple will face during pregnancy is the possibility of miscarriage.

Several months before I became pregnant, I heard the heartbreaking news that a friend's baby had died; she found out at ten weeks. (More of her story can be found in Appendix I.) A D&C (a procedure to remove the baby) followed a few days later. As I watched my friend's heartache unfold on her blog during the next weeks and months, it made me fearful for my own pregnancy.

According to the American Congress of Obstetricians and Gynecologists (ACOG), miscarriage is the most common type of pregnancy loss. The American Pregnancy Association reports:

> Studies reveal that anywhere from 10–25% of all clinically recognized pregnancies will end in miscarriage. Chemical pregnancies may account for 50–75% of all miscarriages. This occurs when a pregnancy is lost shortly after implantation, resulting in bleeding that occurs around the time of her expected period. The woman may not realize that she conceived when she experiences a chemical pregnancy.[1]

Most miscarriages occur during the first thirteen weeks of pregnancy, and the number one cause is chromosomal abnormalities, which cannot be prevented.

Given the statistics, you or someone you are close to has probably experienced losing a baby through miscarriage. The prospect of it can create some anxiety as you go through the early weeks of pregnancy.

My friend Sarah experienced a miscarriage with her first pregnancy. "The first time, we told *everyone*," she says. "After we called family, less than an hour after we had a positive test, we went for a walk and told neighbors we barely knew. I waited until we had a good ultrasound at nine and a half weeks to share the news on Facebook."

They lost the baby at twelve weeks.

"When we found out we were pregnant again, we were very quiet about it," Sarah says. "We didn't even tell our families until eighteen weeks, when we found out his gender. I kept tags on his clothes until thirty-six weeks. I was terrified."

Sarah says God provided specific comfort during that pregnancy. On twelve weeks to the day of her second pregnancy—the day she had miscarried her first baby—a high school friend Sarah hadn't spoken with for ten years sent her a message to say she had been awakened in the middle of the night, prompted to pray for Sarah. "We marveled at God's amazing love for us," Sarah says. "The Lord was such a faithful comfort during that time." Three years later, Sarah has two healthy little boys.

"AS LONG AS THE BABY'S HEALTHY"

When Jason and Kristin headed into the twenty-week ultrasound for their fourth child, they deliberated about whether or not they should find out the gender of the baby. "This is the typical decision a couple makes at this point. Do we find out or not?" Kristin says.

Instead, as the technician guided the ultrasound wand over Kristin's pregnant belly, and the couple watched the monitor, they thought they saw something unusual. The technician explained she'd show the pictures to the doctor, and they could expect to hear from him in a day or two.

"Nothing was said between us," Jason says, "but I think we both saw it. Kristin voiced it when we arrived at her mom's house to pick up the kids. 'I'm just concerned,' she said. 'What if our baby doesn't have legs?'"

The next day the doctor called, but the news was not hopeful. "This was the one that smacked us hard," Kristin says, "the one that took us to the edge of fear and doubt. The beginning was rough."

Initially, the doctors believed the baby might have phocomelia, a condition where the baby's organs and facial features do not develop properly. "It was gut-wrenching," Kristin says. "This was not how our child should be, not how any child should be. But God was there. God was telling us that we had to accept whatever was to come. That this life was one that He was creating for His purposes."

Jason adds: "It was the most powerless feeling to simply have no control over the news or situation unfolding in front of you. It seemed unreal that it was happening at all. But I felt peace somehow. I felt God was still there and that He needed me to carry us through. I knew ultimately, though, it wasn't me at all. He was giving me peace so He could use me."

Dr. Kevin Weary says, "Some of the hardest moments of people's lives are when they find out about something that's wrong in utero." He encourages couples to keep the proper perspective. "If the baby has a club foot, that's not ideal," he says. "That baby's likely going to need surgery. But it's going to be okay.

"Then there are other things that aren't going to change, such as a genetic diagnosis. You thought the baby's chromosomes were going to be one way, and they're not."

A few days after Jason and Kristin learned of their son's potentially devastating condition, they went in for an appointment with a specialist. "We prayed. We walked. We rode the elevator to the fourth floor . . . we waited," the couple wrote on their blog. Jason says dozens of friends and family members were already praying—some not even knowing the situation—and the couple felt those prayers acutely.

View from the Nursery

God Has Answered: My Journey of Infertility

by Sarah Romanov

I held my newborn daughter in my arms, marveling at her dark hair, button nose, and tiny fingers. With a joyful heart, I kissed her soft cheek and breathed in her sweet scent. *It had happened. I was finally a mother!*

I met my husband, Andrew, at Bible college, and we married when I was nineteen. We didn't try to have a baby right away. But after I graduated, we felt the time was right. One year went by, then two . . . then three. And I did not get pregnant.

After our eighth anniversary, we went in for medical tests and were diagnosed with unexplained infertility. We tried the least invasive treatment, unsuccessfully, but didn't feel peace about more involved procedures.

We tried several natural remedies, but we eventually accepted the fact that we might never have children. We gave our desires to God and asked for His will to be done. He graciously gave us peace and a deep trust in His goodness, which sustained us, even while our younger siblings were getting married and giving our parents the grandchildren we had long desired to give them. Even through moments of sadness, God gave me joy in my unfulfilled desires.

Then, a few months after our fourteenth anniversary, Andrew was spending an afternoon praying and journaling when he felt like God gave him the message that I was going to get pregnant soon. When he told me, I wasn't sure what to think. *If we haven't been able to have a baby after all these years, why would it happen now?*

Forty days later, Andrew convinced me to take a pregnancy test—on Labor Day morning—and it was positive!

Because of our years of infertility, my emotions during pregnancy were heightened. When I experienced minor spotting early in my pregnancy, which is common, it scared me. At one point I was crying on the bathroom floor, begging God to let me keep the baby. I feared getting so close to my dream of being a mother only to have it all slip away.

With time, I learned to trust God with each pregnancy-related fear, and I was able to enjoy being pregnant, even though it was surreal. I could hardly believe I got to buy maternity clothes, register for baby items, and attend baby showers given in my honor. It was a joyful time, made all the sweeter by the path we'd traveled to arrive at that point.

When our precious baby was born, we named her Elianna Grace, which means "God has answered." The truth of Romans 12:2—that God's will is "good, pleasing, and perfect"—sustained me during our years of infertility. It also allowed me to rejoice in the new chapter God was writing in our story. God, in His wisdom, sent Elianna at the exact time she needed to be here. And she was worth the wait.

A high-powered ultrasound revealed that the baby did not have phocomelia. The baby also did not have legs. In addition, the baby had an underdeveloped right arm that ended at the elbow and a split hand (a thumb and two larger fingers) on the left arm. Otherwise the baby appeared to be developing normally.

The diagnosis was a rare genetic disorder that had only been reported in as few as five other families around the world.

Jason and Kristin say that an intelligent, motivated doctor was one of the special comforts God provided. Their decision to continue with the pregnancy—a non-decision that stemmed from their belief that life begins at conception—was met with their doctor's "obsessive enthusiasm." As he left no stone unturned in finding a diagnosis, they felt he was on their team. "It felt better to know something," Kristin says of the diagnosis, "and to hear the doctor say our child would have a chance to be born healthy and live."

A short time later, the couple learned they were having a boy. And on a sunny day in May, Dillon came into the world, weighing five pounds and fourteen ounces. Wrapped in a receiving blanket, he looked exactly like any other newborn.

Jason and Kristin knew there would be challenges ahead, raising a child with limb differences (a term used in the limb-loss community). "We weren't scared of Dillon in any way," Kristin says, "but we were scared of how others would treat him—how they would talk about him and notice him."

Dr. Weary points out that no parent knows exactly what challenges might come along with having a child. "The reality is that we never know how that child is going to develop and at what levels they will perform according to the world's standards," he says. "In some circumstances, we know that child will be challenged in ways you didn't plan—whether it be Down syndrome or something else.

"When I sit down with parents receiving this kind of news, I remind them that this child is on purpose. You were chosen to love this child. God thinks you're the right parents."

Jason and Kristin are convinced their family was chosen—and blessed—to love Dillon. "He is such an inspiration to us," Kristin says. "He smiles more than any child I know. He is funny and loves to move and laugh. He crawls, eats by himself, enjoys coloring, and loves to play with his brothers and sister."

The couple has surprisingly normal fears for their son. "We don't want him to be hurt by what others say," Kristin says. "Dillon looks different, and we completely understand the curiosity that comes along with that. We just want him to know God's love and peace in his life, and we want him to feel confident in our love for him."

The couple, who describe themselves as "courageously enabled," say they've made trust in God a priority since the start of their relationship, and that played a large role in how they were able to cope—and even thrive—in the midst of adversity. "While dating we dealt with our pasts, broken families, and issues of forgiveness," Kristin says. "Throughout our marriage God has been leading us and encouraging us, and we've placed our trust fully in Him."

DEALING WITH FEAR

Erin Smalley struggled with fear during her third pregnancy. After surviving a life-threatening case of HELLP syndrome (a complication associated with preeclampsia) at the end of her second pregnancy, Erin went into her third pregnancy with her doctor's blessing—but also with intense fear.

If fear is something you're dealing with, Erin suggests being honest about how you're feeling and voicing your fears to your spouse, a friend, or even a therapist. "Avoid judging your emotions," she says. "Emotions are the voice of your heart. When you verbalize them, you're giving your heart a voice."

In her own case, Erin feared the serious condition would recur, threatening her life or the baby's. "I acknowledged that I was feeling afraid," she says. "Then I battled the fear, because I knew it wasn't from the Lord."

Erin says to combat the anxiety they felt, she and Greg prayed together and asked others to pray for them. She memorized powerful Scripture passages, such as 2 Corinthians 4:8–9, which says: "We are hard pressed on every side, but not crushed; perplexed, but not in despair; persecuted, but not abandoned; struck down, but not destroyed." She also listened to worship music to calm her spirit and keep the right perspective.

"I had to trust that this was God's baby, that the baby's life and my life belonged to Him," she says. "Later there are the teenage years, and then your children go to college. So really learning to trust God with your child is a lesson for life."

When Erin began to swell at the end of her pregnancy, she delivered her third child—a daughter—at thirty-seven weeks. "I ended up having this amazing, healthy baby," she says. "It was just a miracle of God."

LESSON FOR LIFE

For Kevin and me, everything went smoothly with my first pregnancy. The birth was also uneventful; I gave birth naturally following six hours of labor, and our healthy baby boy was born a week before Christmas. We named him Josiah, which means "Jehovah heals."

When our son was seven months old, he suddenly began having seizures. During a weeklong hospital stay, in which he regressed to the development level of a four-month-old, Josiah was diagnosed with a rare and serious form of childhood epilepsy. In some cases, the neurologist explained to us, the seizures could be stopped, and the child would go on to develop normally. In other cases, the child's development would be irreparably stunted. We could only wait and see.

As my husband and I spent sleepless nights in the hospital, I was gripped with fear for my baby. I truly did feel as if my heart was lying there in that hospital crib. And in the months that followed, as Josiah received treatment and began to slowly improve, God taught me what it meant to place my child fully in His loving, capable hands.

I came to understand that God had created my son and had a plan for him. And I realized that my biggest fear was that I would not like God's plan for him as well as my own.

Think about Abraham in the Bible—you know, *Father* Abraham—who was asked to sacrifice his son to demonstrate his faith in God. Not only was Isaac Abraham's child, but he was also the son God had promised to Abraham and given him in his old age. Through this son, God had said, generations would be blessed. I'm sure this daddy wondered, *How could God possibly have a good plan in all of this? I'm really not sure if He has this under control!*

Yet, in faith, as Hebrews tells us, Abraham did the unthinkable. He raised the knife above his own son with the intention of carrying out God's command. And God provided another way.

When Josiah became sick, I think I felt a little bit of what Abraham must have felt. *If my son lived life, staying at a four-month-old level, that was a tragedy, wasn't it? How could that be God's plan?*

But the Lord lovingly helped me and Kevin to see that He not only had it under control but was working things out for our good—as individuals and as a family. I'm not going to lie; this was a painful, gut-wrenching lesson to learn. And I only experienced peace and freedom from fear once I had fully surrendered my baby to God.

At age three, Josiah is walking and talking and catching up with his peers. But he will probably deal with lifelong balance and coordination problems because part of his brain was damaged by the seizures. Sometimes my mind wanders to what might have been, and I ask, "Why couldn't it have been perfect, Lord?"

And He lovingly answers, "It could have been perfect—by your definition—but then it would not have been My will—My good, pleasing, perfect will."

I realize then that the perfection I truly want is the perfection of God's will manifesting itself in our family.

Katie Wetherbee, a popular blogger and former special education teacher, experienced a similar thing when her oldest daughter developed epilepsy the day before she turned five. What followed was a month-long hospital stay and years of rehabilitation.

During that time, Wetherbee took comfort in the knowledge of God's sovereignty. "It's not unexpected to Him," she says. "Nothing at all surprises Him. There were questions I'd ask the doctors, and they'd say, 'I don't know.' I was comforted when they said that because I was more aware that God *did* know."

Of her own journey as a parent (her daughter is now nineteen and a sophomore in college), Wetherbee says, "I wouldn't trade what we went through for the world, because there have been a lot of blessings that have flowed out because God allowed it."[2]

There are many days when I am confronted with old familiar fears for the well-being of my children. Josiah misses a developmental milestone or Sadie gets sick, and my mind jumps to the worst-case scenario. Even watching one of them be shunned by other children or misjudged by an adult can wrench this mama's heart.

When my babies were in the womb, my intense desire was for everything to be "okay," and that feeling has continued, sometimes to an even greater extent, now that they are out in the "real world." I see all too clearly my limitations in protecting them. The opportunity is this: God promises to be our strength and help in every circumstance. That includes the emotional ups and downs of pregnancy and the demands of parenthood. Daily entrusting my children to His care and believing that He has good plans for them are two of the best things about being a parent.

It's common for emotions to run high during this very special time of life. Addressing your fears and other emotions before your baby arrives sets you up for being a parent who trusts in God—the firmest foundation and greatest source of hope available. With Him by your side, the emotional roller coaster of parenthood can be an enjoyable ride.

TIME TO TALK

- What emotions have presented themselves most strongly during your pregnancy?
- What past experiences may contribute to negative emotions you are experiencing, such as fear, anxiety, or worry? (For example, infertility or a past miscarriage.)
- In what ways are you "battling" unhealthy fear? Is there more you could be doing?
- If you have experienced "bad news" about your baby, how have you placed the situation in God's hands?
- Do you find it easy or difficult to give your baby's future over to God's sovereignty? What is something He might be teaching you through this experience?

Pray for God to deepen your trust in Him and His purposes. Give Him permission to use your life and your baby's for His glory. Ask for His "good, pleasing and perfect will" to be manifested in your pregnancy and in the life of your child.

CHAPTER EIGHT

Fitting In and Finding Community

When I became a parent, it never crossed my mind that I might end up with a friend problem. I'd never had trouble making friends, but my journey from being single to married to mommy—all within two years—had caused my social life to suffer. Most of my friends were single and working, which worked out great when I could meet them for lunches and evening coffees. But all of that was about to change.

Although I was excited about the transition, I wasn't prepared for the isolation I would face going from a full-time job to staying home with my baby. I didn't understand how difficult it would be to maintain friendships with people whose social circles I no longer frequented. And when Josiah arrived, I soon learned that I could only survive for so long on Facebook "likes" before I felt like I was stranded on a desert island with only a volleyball . . . excuse me, an infant . . . for company.*

And to be honest, I didn't really know how to engage with the "mommy culture." I felt totally competent meeting with single women and offering them dating advice, or talking to writers about crafting an engaging article, but I felt at a total loss inserting myself into a

---

* In the 2000 movie *Cast Away*, a FedEx employee, played by Tom Hanks, is involved in a plane crash in the South Pacific and spends four years on an island with only a volleyball that he names "Wilson" as his companion.

conversation about what kind of diapers are best. I didn't feel like an expert on being a mom, and that lack of confidence caused me to shy away from connecting with other mommy-types.

Kristy says she experienced something similar. Before her son was born, most of her friends were single. Then as a brand-new mommy, she suffered with postpartum depression. "Having friends helped, but they didn't understand what I was going through," she says. "I resented that I wasn't able to just drop everything and go like I had before I had a baby. I think having other mommy friends in the trenches with me probably would've helped normalize some of the things I was thinking and feeling."

FRIEND TRANSITIONS

Catherine Claire Larson, who left her job of seven years to stay home with her son, says she's thankful she spotted a social change on the horizon.

"I remember a conversation I had with my husband while I was still pregnant," she says. "I told him, 'My peer group is going to be changing a lot in the next year. It's going to go from primarily spending time with my work colleagues to really needing to dig into some new friendships that will be able to gird and guide me in the years ahead.'

"I remember pulling my pregnant belly under the table and saying, 'Can we pray tonight that the Lord would give me some really good new mommy friends that I can call on and learn from?'" Larson says the Lord was faithful to provide those relationships in the form of other moms and mentors. "I'm glad that I had thought about it beforehand and prayed for those relationships," she says.

BE INTENTIONAL

Here's the thing: Community requires effort. As a woman, when you have an infant, joining a small group or even meeting a friend for coffee necessitates coordinating schedules, figuring out childcare, and doing what it takes to get out of the house (in my case, picking out a decent outfit and putting on makeup).

Women aren't the only ones to feel a squeeze on their social lives. My husband says his social life decreased after our son was born because he felt a stronger obligation to be at home, supporting me. "Spending an evening hanging out with a buddy became a luxury I didn't always feel I could afford," he says. "I still don't sometimes."

But the Bible is clear that community needs to be a priority for believers. Consider what Hebrews 10:24–25 has to say: "Let us consider how to stir up one another to love and good works, not neglecting to meet together, as is the habit of some, but encouraging one another, and all the more as you see the Day drawing near" (ESV).

Real Advice for New Parents

When our first daughter was two, our church offered a parenting small group; that was a great benefit to us and the six other couples in our group. It was one of the most fun times we've ever had in a small group. Going through a good, solid parenting curriculum together can highlight some of your initial differences and really put you on the same sheet of music to start off parenting strong.

—*Matt, father of six*

GIRLS NEED GIRLS

Women, in particular, need community with other women—especially in times of great transition. Erin Smalley, who wrote *Grown-Up*

Girlfriends, says: "Female friendship does such amazing things for a woman's personal well-being and her health and wellness. At no other time in life will you need girlfriends as much as with your first child. Hanging out with a girlfriend has been proven to cause a woman's stress to decrease. Even when you are exhausted, tired, and worn out, one of the best things you can do for yourself is go and have a cup of coffee with a friend."

I know from experience that this is something a new mom has to be intentional about. During my son's first six months of life, I rarely got together with girlfriends. I thought I was doing okay and just wanted to spend the evenings with my husband, enjoying our baby together. Over time, this made me extraordinarily dependent on Kevin to meet all of my social and emotional needs—something that was impossible for him to do alone.

And while it may seem counterproductive to make the effort to go out when you're tired and stressed, Erin explains why it's not. "You don't realize how much good going out with a girlfriend will do you," she says. "It's amazing the amount of energy you will regain to take care of your baby and your husband.

"Seek out mature, grace-filled girlfriends who are either sharing the same journey or maybe are one step ahead. Be willing to be vulnerable and share where you are really at emotionally. And call that person in those difficult moments when you need to vent, seek advice, or ask for help or prayer."

Just for Him
His and Hers Community

Dr. Greg Smalley explains that one of the best things a man can do for his wife is make sure she gets some time with her friends. "The man needs to encourage his wife to have friends," he says. "He might be feeling jealous that he's not getting all the attention—and date nights are also important—but Erin and I encourage new dads to do everything in their power to help their wives spend time with friends. She has needs you're not going to be able to meet as a man."

A guy I used to work with would buy his wife gift cards to various coffee shops as Christmas or birthday presents with the specification that they were to be used for "coffee dates" with her girlfriends—babysitting included.

In addition to making sure their wives cultivate friendships, Joshua Rogers says new dads also need community. "Maintaining a social life since my children were born has required me to get creative about when I hang out with my guy friends," he says.

Rogers, who already makes it a priority to go to the gym early each morning, says he has a workout buddy who is in the same stage of life. "This gives us an opportunity to catch up and get healthy at a time when our wives and kids don't need us," he says. "I also schedule lots of lunches with friends (it actually requires a line item in the budget), which has provided countless hours to catch up with friends."

In addition to the gym and lunches, Rogers meets weekly with two other guys to "share the important details of our lives, confess our brokenness, and pray for each other. Basically, I squeeze my guy friends into all the spaces of time where my wife doesn't need me. She appreciates their influence on my life and doesn't feel like she's having to compete for my attention."

TRADING FACEBOOK FOR FACE TIME

Alysia went through a rough transition when her daughter was born. Dealing with a fussy, colicky baby was aggravated by spending time on social networking sites. "People only talk about the good things, not the hard things," she says. "If your friends have 'easy' babies, that's all you hear about. It's hard when you see all these Facebook statuses about perfect babies; you just think, *Must be nice.*"

Alysia says that hearing about other people's positive experiences made her wonder if something was wrong with her baby. When she met another mom (at a moms group at her church) who was going through the same thing, it was a turning point.

"I was blessed to find a fellow 'fussy-baby mommy' to connect with," Alysia says. "It has been a huge blessing to be able to talk about what we're experiencing with our babies and walk through being new moms together."

She says realizing that she's not alone has been helpful and encouraging. "And not believing everything you read on social media is huge," she says. "Everyone always puts their 'best face' out there, but things aren't always as good as they want you to believe."

For men, the biggest social problem may be finding time to spend with their buddies (see suggestions in "His and Hers Community"). Between work and home responsibilities, a guy may feel like there's no time left to connect with other men. When my husband needs some guy time, he often arranges for babysitting so that I can also have a break. Or we take turns watching the kids, so that each of us can spend time with a friend.

MOMS GROUPS

Last year, I decided I needed some "mom" friends (most of my friends were from my single years), so I joined a MOPS (Mothers of Preschoolers) group at my church. Because I don't excel at crafts or homemaking, I was pleasantly surprised that I wasn't required to use a hot glue gun or bake muffins even once. In fact, I enjoyed the encouraging speakers and discussion time with the women at my table.

"Being a mom is a tremendously big job, and it can be very, very scary," says Sherry Surratt, CEO and president of MOPS International. "It's natural to think, *I don't know what I'm doing.* You need people to talk to about your worries who can say, 'I understand, and you're going to be okay.'"

View from the Nursery
From Isolation to Community
by Jill Kinsey Hadley

When my son was four months old, I was a first-time mom in the thick of postpartum depression. I had been unsuccessful in breast-feeding my son, and I struggled with not being able to do something that was supposed to be natural.

For his first six months of life, I used a breast pump four times a day and fed him with a bottle. Although this was beneficial for him, it was isolating for me. With the time it took to pump milk, feed, and change my baby, there was little time remaining to actually get out of the house before the process had to begin again.

Adding to my feelings of isolation, my husband and I had moved five hours away from our family and friends just a year before I became pregnant. And though we had joined a small group at our church, most of the women there were closer to my mom's age than mine.

I first heard about MOPS from my sister-in-law, whose son was a year older than mine. Then a friend at church invited me to attend a meeting with her. I didn't know what to expect when I walked into that first meeting, and I was a little overwhelmed. Getting myself ready and packing up my son and all of his "stuff" required a lot of coordination.

I was immediately greeted by my table's "mentor mom," who showed me where to sit and introduced me to the women at my table. My table leader asked me to come over to her house the very next week—something I will never forget.

After that first meeting, I was sold. I wanted to be part of a group that encouraged me as a first-time mom who felt clueless. The thing that helped me the most during that first year was simply listening to others at my table talk about all that had happened while they were trying to get ready to come to the meeting. It became evident that no matter how crazy I thought my morning was, someone else had a tougher time getting there! There was a sense of camaraderie, and I looked forward to my table leader calling me during the week to check in.

I am in my eighth and final year of MOPS. I have served as a table leader and part of the Steering Team for the past few years. It's been through serving and plan-ning that MOPS has become an integral part of my life. I developed lifelong friendships, and I learned that women need other women. I learned the power of both prayer and laughter. I learned that I was capable of serving and blessing others despite the fact that I didn't have it all together myself.

Surratt points out that mothers of young children face particular challenges other moms do not, such as feedings, nap times, and potty training. "Her life can be isolating as she spends a lot of time in the home, just her and the children," she says. "That raises the need for friendships, connection, help, and advice."

MOPS meetings, which take place on a biweekly basis, consist of a meal or a snack, a speaker, time to chat with other moms, and sometimes a "Pinteresty" project. The ministry of MOPS serves a mom from the time she has a newborn until her youngest child has started school.

"You need to start thinking about a MOPS group while you're expecting," Surratt says. "When you bring your first baby home, you instantly need a support group around you. Mothering is too hard to do alone. And why should you, when there are so many moms out there ready to help?"

The ultimate goal of MOPS, Surratt says, is that moms would take the next step in their relationship with Christ. "My favorite thing about MOPS is that it gives every mom the opportunity to hear about how much God loves her," she says. "God has an incredible plan for her life. Ultimately MOPS is about letting God make us into better moms."

For the reasons I listed earlier, I felt intimidated by moms groups and worried that I wouldn't fit in. Along with MOPS, many churches offer other mom support groups and mentorship opportunities. Find out what your church offers and get involved. You may also want to join a community group, such as Stroller Strides or a library reading group, as a means to form relationships outside of the church.

Julie says that, when she stayed home with her daughter, God led her to a friend right in her own neighborhood. "On one of my first walks around the local park, I met another mom, and we became friends," Julie says. "She and her husband were not Christians, and I prayed for nine years for them to find Jesus—even after they moved away."

Two years ago, Julie was delighted when every member of that family accepted Christ. "I was blessed to be a part of their journey to find Jesus," she says. And it all began with finding a friend.

If you're having a hard time finding a group where you feel like you fit, consider starting your own group. I discovered that because I went from a long-standing career directly to being a stay-at-home mom, I had some specific needs and stresses that many other moms didn't share. Through Facebook I gathered a list of other local women in my same situation, and we began meeting for breakfast once a month. It was a relief and an encouragement to talk to other moms who understood *exactly* what I was going through.

View from the Nursery
A Different Kind of Community
by Elsa Kok Colopy

As a single mom of a toddler, I felt lost.

Life had taken an unexpected turn, and now I was responsible for all the parenting duties on my own—doctor's appointments, bedtime, childcare. I felt broken, helpless, and overwhelmed. Along with that, I faced financial battles, loneliness, and a deep sense of insecurity.

I hadn't been to church in a long time, but one day I walked into a small city church in search of hope and help. God was gracious. He brought some older women into my life who began to teach me about God's character and love for me.

Change didn't come easily. Not everyone was kind toward my situation, and I wasn't always kind to myself. But when I really looked, I could see the grace of God in the eyes of some joyful, contagious believers, and their love for me began to make a difference. I showed up to their Bible studies and let them into my world—as messy as it felt to do so.

I began to grow in my faith, but it was the loneliness that seemed toughest to shake. At night when my daughter was in bed, the quiet of my home felt painfully hollow. I knew I needed more than a once-a-week Bible study—I needed friendship, family, and a place to belong. That hunger drove me to reach beyond myself and invite some other single moms to gather at my home.

It was a big deal to let them see the layers of dust or the sink full of dishes, but that small group of women became my lifeline. We'd get together for dinner and then let the children watch a movie in the bedroom while we talked of life and faith in the living room. God showed up and bonded us together, using us to pour out His love into each other's lives.

During the twelve years I was a single mom, God transformed my family. From showing up to church in search of help, my daughter and I came to a place of helping others. The journey wasn't perfect, but ultimately God took the most challenging circumstance of my life and showed me His heart, His love, and His care in a way that changed everything.

COMMUNITY FOR TWO

Along with seeking out friendship and connection individually, couples should consider engaging in community together. Mark Holmen, founder of Faith@Home Ministries, suggests that parents participate in small groups with other believers. While he recommends that dads and moms seek out community individually, he also encourages couples to attend a group together, if possible.

"When our daughter was a baby, we were in a small group where everyone had just had their first child," he says. "We did life together; we learned together and experienced it together."

Another way new parents can engage in community is to find a mentor couple. When Holmen and his wife were expecting their daughter, he noticed a couple, Dave and Jean, who worked in the youth ministry at his church. They had a good relationship with their teenage daughters, and he thought, *That's what I want!*

Holmen and his wife, Maria, asked the couple to be their daughter's godparents. And through the years, Holmen and his wife would consult Dave and Jean for advice.

"Put your 'go-to' people in place beforehand," Holmen suggests. "You may have your own parents, but sometimes you need that neutral person."

∞

Some of the challenges Kevin and I faced socially when our son was born could have been prevented if we had been proactive about discovering where we would fit in and find community after his birth. Three years later, we're finally being intentional about establishing community—particularly with others in our life stage and those a few steps ahead.

But finding community certainly doesn't require discarding existing friendships. Julie, who had to build a new network of friendships when she left her job to stay home with her first daughter, says, "Ask God to help you cultivate relationships that reflect His heart."

Those friendships may not always be with those in your exact life stage, she says. "I still do coffee with several of my former co-workers regularly—some are single and some are married without children. I also have friends who are better at the homemaking thing than I am, and I've learned aspects of godliness from them, too. Dropping extra requirements for friendships opens up doors when you listen to the Lord."

TIME TO TALK

- Who makes up your primary community—both individually and as a couple—right now? Do you anticipate that changing when the baby is born?
- Do you need to invest in some new friendships to ensure that you have community following your child's birth?
- What are some ways you can engage in community as a couple?
- How can you be proactive now to make sure both of you have community and friendship following your baby's birth?
- Are there any doors for friendship or community that you may have not considered?

Take some time to pray about the relationships God has for you as you enter into this new season of life. Ask Him to provide friends and mentors who can support and encourage you.

CHAPTER NINE

Parents in Training

When I was single, I had this idea that I'd turn into a different person when I got married. I'd be more domestic and given to fits of hospitality. I'd be gentler and possess more wisdom. I'd spend more time being productive and less time watching TV.

Essentially, I imagined my flaws would be gone, or greatly decreased, and I would have a whole new set of "wifely" characteristics.

Kevin imagined that he would stay the best version of himself— that the sweeping romantic gestures he made while we were dating would continue on into infinity. And obviously he would always hang on my every word and stare deeply into my eyes without distraction. "I thought that as my wife's knight in shining armor, my armor would always shine," he says.

Our glorified views of our own marital success didn't happen . . . exactly.

Despite that fact, the transition into being husband and wife was fairly seamless. We were still ourselves (which was good, since we each remained the person the other had fallen in love with), just with new roles and responsibilities.

Sure, I had to learn some new things—like how to provide dinner for a hungry man each night (cereal just wasn't going to cut it), but for the most part, I continued to be me. And I happily discovered that I could actually use some of my talents to bless Kevin. I helped him write a cover letter that got him an interview for a job he really wanted and eventually got. I applied my communication skills to listen to him verbally process his day and offer him counsel. And my naturally laid-back and fun-loving disposition, which was similar to his, allowed us to enjoy refreshing evenings together after busy workdays.

The downside of continuing to be me was that I did not magically develop the skill set of a wife—or at least the skill set I believed a wife should possess—skills like planning and preparing healthy meals, keeping Kevin's shirts ironed, and making our house a home.

In fact, our first Christmas together, Kevin helped me create a beautiful nativity scene on the mantel, complete with snowy flocking, and we turned our modest townhome into a Christmas wonderland. When my mom came to visit—her first visit since I'd married—she remarked, "Wow! This place looks better than it ever has."

After a quick pause, I quipped, "I guess it just needed a man's touch."

The point is, I didn't excel at home décor or gourmet cooking before marriage, and I didn't naturally master these things because I became a wife. Things I had struggled to be disciplined doing as a single continued to be a challenge. And activities I didn't enjoy doing before marriage didn't magically become my new favorites.

Kevin experienced a similar reality check. "Going back to the example of a knight in shining armor," he says, "I didn't realize I'd have to polish my armor so often. The pressure of putting someone else's needs ahead of my own 24/7 could be exhausting. Work distractions, laziness, and selfish desires dulled my armor. I quickly realized it was going to take effort to keep it shiny."

Then came parenthood.

Similar to becoming husband and wife, Kevin and I assumed that when our baby arrived, we would become different people. Well, or at least some parental superpowers would kick in. I would suddenly be overtaken with motherly instinct and love caring for this tiny person, and Kevin (who *loves* to sleep) would eagerly rise at all hours of the night to help me care for our precious bundle.

I'd heard of such things happening. One new mom I know posted on Facebook one week into motherhood: "I finally feel like I am doing what God created me for." *That's* what I expected to feel.

Another friend told me, "I'm only two weeks in, but so far motherhood is the most miraculous experience of my life."

And she's not wrong. There are certain wonderful perks to the job of being a mom (or a dad). Among the most satisfying for me is going into my son's room first thing in the morning. He practically bursts with joy at the sight of me, eager to give me hugs and kisses. No human in my entire life has been *that* excited about me (though my husband has come close). I enjoy this part of motherhood because it revolves around relationship.

Similarly, Kevin loves coming home at the end of a workday and having our eighteen-month-old daughter crawl up into his lap to tell him a story in gibberish.

Unfortunately, neither of us relishes the manual labor part.

My sister-in-law, Anna, on the other hand, truly doesn't mind cutting fruit into little pieces, reading children's books, and wiping little noses. Describing her experience of staying home with her first baby, she says, "I enjoyed holding him, cuddling him, and being close to him. Even changing diapers and cleaning up *all* of the spit-up were just matter-of-fact chores that needed to be done, and I never really tired of them."

I did. In fact, the daily "mechanics" of being a mom is where my enthusiasm for parenting wanes. I vividly remember one Saturday morning when my son was six months old. Missing my pre-baby Saturday morning routine of sipping a cup of coffee while catching up on reality TV shows, I strapped that little towhead into his high chair, sprawled dramatically on the couch, and moaned, "I don't *want* to feed him."

Baby Shopping List

The list of things you *could* buy for your new little one is endless. But remember, you really only need a few things right at the beginning. In addition, parents vary on what they consider essential. Some couldn't live without the scented diaper bin, while others find it a waste of money and space. I depended on my changing table, but some moms prefer the mobility of a changing pad.

Try interviewing a few parents of young children to find out what you *really* need during those first few months.

Here's a basic list to get you started:

1. Infant car seat*
2. First outfits (between ten and twenty changes of clothes)
3. Diapers and wipes
4. Crib, bassinet, or co-sleeper
5. Receiving blankets
6. Rubbing alcohol (for umbilical-cord care)
7. Infant bathtub
8. If breast-feeding: nursing bra, nursing pads, and nipple cream
9. If bottle-feeding: bottles, nipples, and bottlebrush
10. Stroller or sling

* You will not be allowed to take your baby home from the hospital without a car seat. Be sure to practice installing it ahead of time to save hassle and stress on the day you go home.

Baby feedings aren't my thing.

My husband reminded me that I did, in fact, need to feed our offspring, and he then served me by doing the job himself. There have been times where I think both Kevin and I have felt like failures as parents or like we're not up to the task. But then I remember that God gave me my husband and children for a specific reason—so that we could bring Him glory as a family.

THE "SUCCESSFUL" FAMILY

Roy Baldwin, director of Parenting and Youth at Focus on the Family, says it's common for parents to doubt their parenting abilities or worry they're going to mess up their kids. "But that kind of thinking is void of the understanding that we have a Creator who loves us and has designed us and realizes that we have our flaws," he says. "We need to take ownership. Our role is to do life with our kids imperfectly—but to God's glory."

Baldwin, who spent twenty years working with at-risk youth, notes that intentionality seems to be the main factor that separates on-track families from those who end up in broken places.

Many of the families he worked with during his time at group homes were not all that different from the families he encountered at church on Sunday or even his own family at times. He realized that the majority of those parents loved their children and had started out with good intentions and great hopes for their families.

"There was some kind of life situation or circumstance that created a massive stress point in their family, and they weren't able to overcome it," he says.

This discovery led Baldwin to study what makes a family successful from God's perspective. He says while it doesn't reference parenting specifically, Ephesians 4:1–3 provides a starting point for defining a successful family:

> I urge you to live a life worthy of the calling you have received.
> Be completely humble and gentle; be patient, bearing with
> one another in love. Make every effort to keep the unity of the
> Spirit through the bond of peace.

Just as each Christ-follower has received a calling, each family has also received a calling, Baldwin says. "What's beautiful is that this looks different from family to family because our callings are all different."

Families must also seek to continually develop the characteristics mentioned in the Ephesians passage—humility, gentleness, patience, long-suffering, and love.

"That's the kind of home we should strive for," Baldwin says. "I need to approach my wife and children with patience and love and aim for maintaining unity of the Spirit and the bond of peace in our home. When we're in alignment with His call and His will, things fall into place, and we find favor."

Jim Daly, president of Focus on the Family, adds: "I think it's important for new parents to remember that 'successful' parenting is not perfect parenting. Every family has issues; every parent makes mistakes. Parenting seems much more manageable when we abandon the idea of doing it right every time. That's an unattainable standard.

"At the same time, I think moms and dads should certainly set goals for themselves as new parents. First and foremost, they should resolve to be an active and constant presence in their kids' lives. Too many of us get caught up in careers, responsibilities, and the rat race, and we miss the chance to truly be there for our kids when it matters."

Forty Developmental Assets

In 1989, the Search Institute found that forty factors contributed to the development of healthy, caring, and responsible young adults. These elements include:

- Family support
- Positive family communication
- Service to others
- Religious community
- Time at home
- Planning and making decisions
- Integrity
- Sense of purpose

Roy Baldwin says his team uses this tool to help parents be intentional about raising children who will avoid problem behaviors as they grow and become healthy, capable, motivated adults.

"The Search Institute surveyed more than 3 million children," Baldwin says. "The more of these forty assets a child has, the research found, the more leadership the child showed, and the healthier his or her relationships were."

Instead of seeing the assets as pressure to complete a checklist, Baldwin suggests that parents think of the list as a starting point for the good things they desire to build into their kids. "These things are intuitive," he says. "What if God designed you to be able to provide these elements? Truth is truth, and God designed it."

For more information on the forty assets, go to http://www.capablekids.com/.

FAITH AT HOME

The moment my son was born, I realized my greatest fear in life: that he might not accept Jesus as his Savior. I felt a sense of terror and help-lessness at the lack of control I had over one of my child's most impor-tant life decisions. My husband and I had brought into the world a soul with a free will to either respond to or reject God's offer of salvation.

While conducting research among expectant parents for this book, I learned that one of the top fears of first-time Christian moms is that their children will rebel as teenagers. Talk about thinking ahead! But I can relate. Like many things in life—finding a spouse, securing a ful-filling career, not getting cancer—I find myself wishing that there was a step-by-step formula for ensuring that my children will love Jesus.

Instead, as Baldwin pointed out, the Bible provides major prin-ciples, but each parent and family must figure out how to enact them.

Mark Holmen, founder of Faith@Home Ministries and the Ex-treme Family Makeover parenting seminar, emphasizes that parents need to concentrate on their own spiritual health in order to pass on faith to their children.

"The research shows that Mom and Dad are going to be two to three times more influential than anything else when it comes to spiri-tual development," he says. "As the parent's faith goes, so goes the faith of the child. For a lot of people, Christianity is a one-hour thing; it's not something that is lived. It needs to be a 24/7 lifestyle, not just going to church on Sunday morning. We need to be in a place where we truly love God with our heart, soul, mind, and strength and where we're connected with other believers."

Small groups and meeting with mentors are two ways Holmen suggests that couples build community with other believers. But even with a great support system, he says, the responsibility of spiritually guiding your children can be daunting. "Don't feel like you have to get it all straightened out before you have a child," he says. "A lot of times, you straighten it out after you have a child. It's good for your kids to see you grow and see you change. Continue to follow God's lead and get better—get stronger."

And don't underestimate the power of a little training. One study found that parents who take parenting classes produce better outcomes in their children than those who don't receive such training—and the more training and education, the better the outcomes.[1]

Praying for Baby

Amber and her husband, Dan, pray for their soon-to-be-born son every day. "When we pray, our hearts become more connected to and invested in him," Amber says. It's never too early to begin praying for your child. Here are a few specific things to bring before the Lord:

- Pray that your son or daughter will trust the Lord (see Psalm 40:4).
- Pray that your child will love God's Word and know His ways (see John 14:26).
- Pray that your son or daughter will grow in the wisdom and knowledge of God (see Ephesians 1:17).
- Pray that your child will feel God's love (see John 15:9).
- Pray that your son or daughter will have a repentant heart (see Psalm 51:17).
- Pray that God's peace will guard your child's heart and mind (see Philippians 4:7).

Along with parenting seminars, Faith@Home provides parenting booklets for moms and dads that include specific instructions on establishing a faith culture in the household in areas such as family devotions and prayer.

LEADING SPIRITUALLY

Right now the biggest parenting concerns on your mind probably revolve around feeding options and choosing the right diapers. The real work of spiritually guiding your child is still a few years away. That doesn't mean it's too early to begin thinking about your strategies and setting a foundation.

Dr. Tedd Tripp, author of *Shepherding a Child's Heart*, suggests an approach to parenting that gets to the heart of the matter.

"In shepherding the heart of my child, I'm not just concerned about managing behavior, but also about helping my child understand the heart issues—the things going on inside those push and pull behaviors," Dr. Tripp says. "As Christians we have incredibly rich resources for understanding motivations. The Bible helps us discern the thoughts and attitudes of the heart."

Dr. Tripp suggests helping even very young children to understand sinful attitudes, such as pride, selfishness, and envy, by speaking "the language of the heart."

"Think of a three-year-old who knocks over his younger sister and takes her toy," he says. "Obviously that's behavior that needs to be corrected, but instead of just saying, 'No, no! That's bad,' I can use the language of the heart and say, 'You're not being kind. You're only loving you; you're not loving her.'

"As I use those biblical ideas to help children understand what's motivating them, it powerfully opens up the way for the gospel as I point them to Christ as the forgiver of sins."

An added benefit of this approach, Dr. Tripp says, is that parents develop solidarity with the child in their shared sinfulness. "There's no sin my children commit that I'm not familiar with myself," he says. "I know every sin that they do personally. The reason I can face those struggles is because God sent His Son into the world to die to forgive me. And there's grace and forgiveness—for me and my child."

Dr. Tripp says that while a young child may not fully grasp the concepts you're reinforcing, you are creating a foundation for teaching biblical truth and revealing who God is as your child grows.

"How we talk about God is such an important aspect of parenting," Dr. Tripp says. "We need to bring the greatness of God and His attributes to our kids. We should be dazzling them with who God is and deepening that as they get older."

At Sonrise Mountain Ranch, nestled deep in the mountains of Colorado, Matt McGee and his wife, Chantal, encourage couples who attend their marriage and family camps to consider what will matter to them at the end of their lives. They call this exercise "The View from the Rocking Chair" (which is also the title of McGee's book), because they ask people to visualize sitting on a porch in a rocking chair at the end of their lives and asking, "With most of my life behind me, what will be most important?"

"When people slow down to take stock of what will be most significant to them in the future, it's the relationships with their spouse and with their children—and those people's relationships with the Lord," McGee says.

Every choice a person makes, he says, no matter how small, costs something. "Someone said the great American lie is that you can be it all, you can do it all, you can have it all," he says. "There are not too many parents I've met who believe that. They realize—and sometimes it's a hard realization—that something will suffer based on their choices. The question is: What will it be?"

McGee says he encourages parents to decide what their top priorities will be and then make daily decisions that reflect those values. "God's got the plan," he says. "He's not saying, 'You come up with the plan.' He knows what we're supposed to do with our marriage and with our kids. Our job is to receive and say, 'We commit to His plan.'"

Real Advice for New Parents

As parents, my wife and I try to make what we call "story decisions." We bought an old house in an older neighborhood because the kids could walk to school. Could we have bought a slightly newer or bigger house? Yeah, maybe. But the story they're going to tell in their thirties is, "We used to be able to walk to school." The story they're *not* going to tell is, "We grew up with ample closet space."

Parent in a way that creates the kind of story you want your children to tell.

—*Jon Acuff, father of two*

MAKING A PARENTING PLAN

Greg Gunn of Family-iD has helped hundreds of families write their own individual "mission and vision statement."

"As a businessman I knew the incredible importance of having a business plan," he says, "a strategy that allowed everyone in the company to be on the same page. Having written goals helped me run an effective business. But somehow I thought the things I wanted to have happen at home would just happen by accident with no plan, strategy, or effort."

Once he discovered this disconnect, Gunn not only wrote a mission statement for his own family, but he founded Family-iD to help other families do the same. He says research shows that people are more likely to accomplish their goals when they write them down. "And if the vision comes from God," he says, "there's a 100 percent chance you'll accomplish it."

Gunn suggests that couples write down specific characteristics they would like to see in their future family. "It's like an artist's rendering of what you want this building to look like," he says.

Family-iD has been helping families put their mission, vision, and values in writing for seventeen years. Gunn says, "Vision creates passion. Passion gives you power to be disciplined. And discipline gives you the courage to totally commit."

Gunn has a hard time not getting carried away when he begins talking about his own family's mission statement, which has come to fruition as his children have grown into teenagers. "We wrote down fifteen qualities we wanted our children to have by the time they were fifteen. We were laughing while we were writing them, thinking, *There's no way!* And they became those things. If you write it down, and God's behind it, it will happen." (A free video and workbook for creating a family mission statement are available at Family-iD.com.)

Uncovering the plans God has for you as parents is an exciting endeavor. At times, it will also be messy, uncomfortable, and stretching. "You're going to have to learn to serve like you've never served before," says author Gary Thomas. "Your heart is vulnerable and exposed like it has never been before. You learn to care for someone like you've never cared before.

"If we embrace this, it really does finish the work of marriage. You learn how to love this child, faults included. Parenthood calls us to even deeper Christlikeness."

Matt McGee adds, "The best seminary in the world is having

children. I've learned more about God and His love for me through having children and watching what they do and my reaction to them." In our three years of being parents, Kevin and I have discovered that we are still ourselves. (You wouldn't believe how comforting that is at times!) While there are days I long to be supermom—and I'm sure Kevin longs to have the shiniest armor on the block—I know God created me with my strengths and weaknesses, just as He created my husband with his. And here's the amazing thing: God has chosen our children to receive both the good and bad of *us*. I don't have to be someone I'm not. I am fully myself—and I am fully a parent. The two don't have to be separated.

Perhaps God knows that our children need more communication and goofy playtime with Mommy and Daddy and less of a variety of solid foods or enriching art projects. Not only does He know exactly what our children need, He has also chosen my husband and me to be the ones who will have the greatest earthly influence on who they become.

That doesn't mean I'm not trying to grow and improve in my areas of weakness; I am. And marriage and motherhood are precisely the things God is using to force me out of my comfort zone and take me to the next level. But I'm also very aware that He knows what He's doing in giving me precisely the husband and the children He has. He knows your family, too, and the kind of parent He's created you to be. The parent only *you* can be.

TIME TO TALK

- What are some characteristics you possess that you believe will serve you well as a parent?
- What are some areas where you feel you are lacking or wish to improve?

• What are some ways you can strengthen your faith as you prepare for parenting?
• Write down some of the values you would like your future family to embody. What are your top five priorities for your marriage and family?
• At the end of your life, what will be most important to you? How can you begin living in a way that moves you closer to your desired outcome?

Reflect on the amazing fact that God has chosen you to be a parent! Ask that He would help you to be intentional in your parenting and that you would be in receiving mode as He reveals His plans to you.

CHAPTER TEN

Roots

When Kevin and I learned I was pregnant, we were thrilled. Both of us were blessed to grow up in Christian homes with parents who loved the Lord and each other. And we were both close to our siblings. That added up to us sharing a very positive view of family life.

In fact, atypical for his gender, Kevin had dreamed about having a wife and children since he was thirteen. And once we were married and people started asking us how many children we planned to have, he would often quip, "Seven!" With solid modeling from our families of origin, we felt nothing but excitement about watching how God would build *our* family.

The morning Skye found out she was pregnant was the day of her husband's alma mater's first football game of the season. Just before kickoff, she presented her husband, Hunter, with a special gift—a baby outfit sporting the college's mascot, a tiger. As Hunter held that tiny outfit, he says he was both excited and scared.

"I've wanted to be a dad for as long as I can remember," he says. "I'm excited to be able to build sofa forts and ambush him with water balloons after school. I'm looking forward to hearing about his day and what he's learning. I'm excited to pass on 'dad wisdom' and see him grow up. But I'm really scared because I don't have a measuring stick of any kind."

Hunter was raised by a single mom after his dad passed away from cancer when Hunter was four. Skye lost both of her parents to a car accident when she was young, so her grandmother raised her. Because of their lack of a traditional family upbringing, the couple says they felt a little adrift when they learned they would be parents.

Skye, who was brought up in an abusive environment, says she knows what *not* to do. "But that doesn't mean that I know what *to* do," she says. "I have been fortunate throughout different stages of my life to have 'adoptive mothers'—women who have come alongside me to love me and emotionally nurture me."

Still, both Skye and Hunter feel as if their biggest obstacle going into parenthood is that each of them lacked a personal example of a two-parent home. "This is uncharted territory for us," Hunter says. "That's exciting as well as scary."

There are many reasons soon-to-be parents may find themselves feeling ill-equipped for the job. Some may feel as if circumstances from childhood will doom them to repeat the same patterns in their own families. Or perhaps they feel uncertain of where to even begin in establishing a whole and healthy family unit.

Whether you have a dramatic story of a painful childhood, or you grew up in what you consider to be a fairly "normal" family, taking a look at your roots can be one of the most helpful exercises as you step into parenthood.

Roy Baldwin says, "Family of origin has a lot to do with how we raise our own kids. In most cases we're either validating what our parents did, or we're reacting to what they did."

Baldwin encourages couples to be self-aware about the messages— true and untrue—that they may have received as a result of their families of origin and how those messages affect their current relationships.

"What are the messages you're constantly replaying in your head?"

he asks. "If my wife and I have a conflict, I may think, *I'm good for nothing*. Where does that come from? I might have heard that during my childhood."

Baldwin suggests that couples be open with one another about these discoveries and not resort to blaming the other person's family. "Try to recognize that your parents likely did the best they could with the situation they had," he says. "No family is perfect."

The truth is, even good parents sometimes make the wrong calls, which means that even the best of families will end up with some mild dysfunction. I recently saw an online list of things no one tells you about before becoming a parent. Number one on the list was, "At some point you will accidentally hurt your kid and feel like the worse parent ever." A cringe-worthy video clip of a woman falling on an air mattress and launching her toddler off the bed, Olympic ski-jump-style, accompanied the list item.[1]

I can relate. There have been moments of parenting when, after the fact, I can only utter, "I can't believe I did that!" Take, for instance, the time I carried my sleeping two-month-old son, strapped in his car seat, into a restaurant to have lunch with a friend. Only after I returned home did I realize that I had unbuckled him under his fleece blanket at the restaurant and then driven him all the way across town in that precarious condition. I felt so terrible I didn't even want to confess to Kevin what I had done.

All parents make mistakes.

Thankfully, many mistakes parents make are easily survived. My mom tells of the time she accidentally ran the diaper pin through the cloth diaper *and* a flap of my brother's skin. She was only alerted to her mistake several minutes later by his persistent crying. She felt terrible, but he survived.

Some mistakes parents make are a little harder to overcome. Deep emotional wounds can continue to fester into adulthood and even impact how you treat your own children.

Justine says a tumultuous childhood with an abusive alcoholic father and a verbally abusive mother played a huge role in her own parenting experience.

"When my first daughter, Kaylee, was born, I asked God to show me how to be a good parent," Justine says. "That was something I had never seen on a day-to-day basis. Even though I had become a Christian, I still had some of the same traits as my parents. When I was angry, I said cutting things to my husband, and sometimes I even swore or threw things like shoes."

Justine's husband came from a stable, healthy Christian family, and he helped her find more constructive ways to express what she was feeling. "But I knew motherhood was a whole new level of responsibility. My husband was mature enough to handle me at my worst, but my children wouldn't understand my behavior."

With her daughter's arrival, Justine continued to struggle with anger. "When I first held Kaylee, I thought I just loved her too much to ever be angry with her," she says. "But that first sleepless week, I found that my exhaustion, frustrations, and fears all came out as anger."

Many nights, after her colicky baby finally fell asleep, Justine would go outside and hit something or yell. "I realized I really needed to change," she says. "I had just as much potential to be violent as my parents had. I couldn't stand the thought of hurting my little girl the way my parents had hurt me, so I cried out to God. The hardest part of changing was slowly going through every painful childhood memory with the Lord and examining it. I had to forgive my parents for things I had tried very hard to just forget. My goal changed from 'Be a better parent than my parents' to 'Keep in conference with God—every minute, every decision.'"

UNTANGLING YOUR ROOTS

Before Baby arrives, it may be helpful for you to consider as a couple how the families you grew up in affect your own thinking and behaviors. For example, you might discover that your family tended to react in anger in stressful situations or struggled to resolve conflicts in a healthy way.

Even differences in "family traditions" can create tension as couples decide what their own family unit will look like. One difference that Kevin and I discovered once our son was born centered around holiday traditions.

I grew up in a family that didn't believe in Santa Claus. My parents allowed Santa to be a fun part of the Christmas season, but they never encouraged us to believe in him. When I asked them about his existence—probably around seven years old—they gave me an honest answer that he was a fun myth that people choose to celebrate at Christmas. Like many Christian families, mine emphasized the birth of Jesus over cultural practices, and from the time I was old enough to question, I knew Santa wasn't real.

Kevin's parents, however, perpetuated a belief in Santa to a much later age with their children. And while they also made Jesus the main focus of the holiday, my husband claims that some of his best childhood memories have to do with believing in the Jolly Old Elf and the whimsical hijinks his parents pulled to convince him and his siblings of Santa's existence.

While this may seem like a minor difference, it continues to be a point of discussion for us as we think about how we will raise our own children. Both of us have warm and wonderful Christmas memories from our childhoods, and both of us grew up with strong family connections and a solid belief in Jesus. In other words, we both feel that our own family's "way" didn't harm us and actually made our lives better.

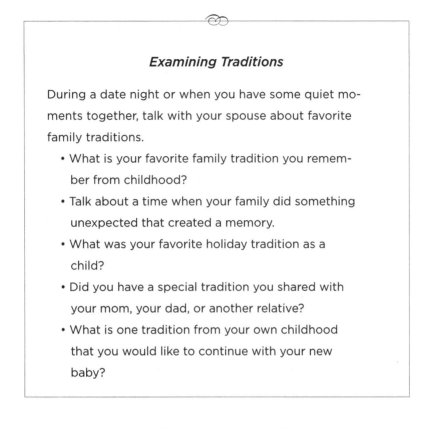

Examining Traditions

During a date night or when you have some quiet moments together, talk with your spouse about favorite family traditions.

- What is your favorite family tradition you remember from childhood?
- Talk about a time when your family did something unexpected that created a memory.
- What was your favorite holiday tradition as a child?
- Did you have a special tradition you shared with your mom, your dad, or another relative?
- What is one tradition from your own childhood that you would like to continue with your new baby?

While the issue of affirming the existence of Santa Claus (or not) is rather minor, consider some other talking points you may encounter:

- Who will be the stay-at-home parent (if either of you)?
- How will the duties of caring for the new baby be shared?
- What spiritual activities will be a priority (baby dedication, christening, church attendance, family devotions, etc.)?
- How will you discipline your child?

As you openly discuss your values and expectations for your future family, decide which standards are sacred and which are negotiable. As long as a practice isn't a biblical mandate, it should be open for discussion.

THE BEAUTIFUL IMPERFECT FAMILY

The "perfect" family is a myth. A casual glance at the Bible shows that even some of our inspired examples had major issues. And yet God used them to do His work and reflect some of His deepest attributes.

The prophet Hosea's love for his unfaithful wife, Gomer, provided a picture of how God unflinchingly loves His people even when they are rebellious and hurtful. The story of the prodigal son demonstrates the committed love of our heavenly Father. And the epic tale of Joseph and his cruel brothers reveals God's forgiveness and sovereignty in the midst of jealousy and dysfunction.

Long before I was married, I heard a speaker say this about marriage: "Some marriages will be easy. Some marriages will be difficult. But both can bring glory to God."

The same is true of families. Some will be fraught with challenges, while others will seem to coast along with little effort. Either way, God promises that He will work every joyful and painful moment together for the good of those who love Him and are called according to His purpose (Romans 8:28). That doesn't mean that everything that happens is good—only that God can redeem everything and use it for His glory.

Maybe you're looking forward to some of the painful circumstances you grew up with being redeemed in your own family. First-time dad Drew is excited to be the "daddy" to his daughter that his wife, Tonya, never had.

Tonya explains, "My biological father left when I was four years old, and I was very much a 'daddy's girl.'" Her father's departure was devastating for Tonya, even though her mom remarried a kind, devoted man. "He didn't have to stick around after my mom died when I was nineteen," she says of her stepdad, "but he did. As wonderful as he is, though, he is not a very emotional man, and I never felt like I could curl up in his arms and break down.

"The struggles I've experienced in my adult life stem partially from a fear of abandonment because of my dad leaving. Drew is sensitive and the kind of dad who will share his emotions with his children—he's what I consider to be a 'daddy.' "

Tonya already sees the bond developing between Drew and their infant daughter, Izzy. "While I have a great stepdad, I missed having a daddy," Tonya says. "Watching Drew with our daughter redeems that for me. He is her daddy, and I feel it healing a part of my heart that ached for that."

Jim Daly, president of Focus on the Family, experienced a tumultuous childhood. Abandoned by his alcoholic father at age five and orphaned by his mother's death from cancer when he was nine, Daly struck out on his own when he was only seventeen. Daly explains that his difficult childhood has given him a passion to live out God's best for his own family.

"Growing up in a dysfunctional environment helped me learn to be a better parent by consistently showing me what not to do," he says. "It instilled in me a strong desire to provide a healthy, safe, stable childhood for my own boys, and to do everything I can to allow them to experience all the things I missed out on when I was growing up."

As Daly's story demonstrates, God is capable of redeeming the roughest of childhoods and even providing divine parenting lessons in the process.

UNPACKING FAMILY BAGGAGE

Sometimes the birth of a child can intensify bad experiences from the father's or mother's own childhood. Joshua Rogers says the birth of his first child stirred up the lack of forgiveness he felt toward his dad.

"When he didn't even suggest the possibility of making a trip to see his new grandchild, it pricked a nerve," Rogers says. "He missed out on a great deal of my childhood when he repeatedly left my mom to go work through his issues, and I felt like his irresponsibility as a dad was replaying itself all over again." Rogers was able to confront his father about his apparent lack of interest in connecting with his new granddaughter.

"It led to an intense conversation during which I also talked to him about the ways it hurt to grow up as his son. He was incredibly receptive and—most importantly—repentant. Within a few weeks, he made the 1,500-mile trip to see his granddaughter (and his son), and it marked a new, healthier chapter in our relationship, which continues to grow."

FORGING A NEW PATH

You are creating a new family. The good news is, regardless of how great or not-so-great *your* family experience was, you can do this family thing however you want. The family God is creating through you is a fresh start, a clean slate.

Leon, the father of eight daughters, says the story of his childhood is not one that, at first glance, would translate to a strong desire for family and fatherhood.

His parents divorced when he was very young, and his mom remarried a man who was verbally and emotionally abusive. "Home was chaotic," Leon says. "My growing-up years were a mixture of love, uneasiness, discomfort, and insecurity. And yet, for some reason, I always wanted to be a dad. Something kept telling me that there must be a better way."

Leon says he paid attention to healthy but realistic examples of marriage. "I noticed couples who argued but loved each other," he says.

"I saw men who struggled at times to provide for their families or relate to their wives but still maintained their commitment to their families. They showed me that imperfect people can stay committed to each other with God's help, which gave me immeasurable hope."

Leon admits there were some obstacles to overcome when his first daughter was born, including laying aside his fear of failure or repeating history. "My wife grew up in an intact family, so she was unfamiliar with the pains of divorce from a child's perspective," he says. "Marrying into my family meant watching me—and helping me—deal with insecurities, stresses, and emotions that were not easy for her to understand."

As he became a father, he says he also had to accept the reality that he was going to struggle with some of the same issues his parents had struggled with, such as anger and harsh words. "I couldn't just declare myself to be different from them," he says. "I needed to recognize that I was susceptible to the same temptations, the same shortcomings, and the same relational problems that were modeled for me growing up."

Still, Leon recognizes a positive side to growing up in a broken home. "One of the greatest takeaways from my childhood is my understanding of the forgiveness and grace required to make family life work. Even as a child, I realized that I needed to have a resilient heart and be willing to forgive even great pains inflicted on me. Now, as a husband and father, I lean on the grace and resiliency of my children and wife as well, and I make it a priority to say 'I'm sorry' when I mess up."

REDEEMING YOUR ROOTS

Despite growing up in a broken home, Joshua Rogers has watched his own family flourish. "One thing I didn't anticipate was how much my kids would adore my wife and me as a couple," he says. "My three-year-old is always saying that I'm the prince and mommy's the princess; she's fixated on our separate roles as husband and wife, mommy and daddy.

Both of our girls are happiest when all four of us are together. When we're all together, my three-year-old gleefully exclaims, 'It's all four of us!'

"Coming from a broken home, I always felt a little defensive of single-parent homes, and I was jaded about the importance of nuclear families. When I heard people talk about the importance of having a mother and father in the home, it just sounded like a somewhat-true conservative talking point. Now that I'm raising two girls in a nuclear family, I'm seeing one of the main reasons that it's so important—because it's important to *them*."

Whatever you experienced in your family of origin will affect your new family and how you parent. Understanding how your background contributes to the type of parent you will be is helpful, but your childhood experiences don't have to define you or your new family. Isaiah 43:19 says, "See, I am doing a new thing! Now it springs up; do you not perceive it? I am making a way in the desert and streams in the wasteland."

Skye, who says she is more excited every day to meet her son, realizes that dealing with her past isn't something she can do in a day. "I don't even know what to do to make up for that sense of 'not being enough' and profound loss," she says. "I know I am on a healing journey and that I need to take one step at a time, one day at a time—trusting that while the wounds run deep, they will heal."

Real Advice for New Parents

Don't compare your babies to anyone else's. Every situation is different. But take advice from those who have been there, even if you think you have it all figured out and read all the right books. Chances are you could learn from them.

—*Tiffany, mother of three*

Chrystal Evans Hurst knows about starting out from a difficult place. At nineteen, she was a brand-new single parent trying to complete college. She gives this advice for overcoming flawed circumstances. "You have the complete ability to make your experience as a parent what you want it to be," she says. "Regardless of your situation—the pregnancy is earlier than planned, it's unplanned, you're by yourself, maybe you're not with the guy—from this point forward you get to choose. You get to choose what kind of parent you're going to be. You get to choose what kind of childhood you're going to give your baby."

Hurst points out that many adults she knows didn't have an ideal childhood or a perfect family, but "when they reflect on their childhood, what they remember is a parent who was happy. A parent who made the best of situations. A parent who knew how to celebrate special events. We create healthy kids by giving the best we can out of what we have to give."

Keep in mind that God knows about all of the broken places in our lives, and He desires to bring restoration. No challenge is too difficult for Him to overcome. No past is too messed up for Him to redeem. And nothing is so lost that He cannot restore it. That truth can allow you to go forward into parenthood with confidence, joy, and hope!

TIME TO TALK

- How would you describe the family you grew up in?
- What are some aspects of your family of origin that could potentially trip you up as you take on the role of parenthood?
- What characteristics of your original family would you like to continue in your own family? Which would you like to leave behind?

- What is something your original family taught you about what makes family life successful?
- What are some all-new dreams that you have for your new family?

Take some time to discuss or journal about some of the realities of the family you grew up in. Talk about some things you appreciate and some things you wish had been different. Ask God to redeem your roots as you set a course for your own family unit.

CHAPTER ELEVEN

Preparing for D-Day

The nursery was painted, the furniture in place, the first outfits and blankets laundered. Over the fireplace—between the stocking embossed with the letter *S*, and its twin embossed with *K*—we hung a third stocking—this one with the letter *J*. No one but us knew our son's name yet: Josiah.

After eight months of eager anticipation, I would be induced the next morning. Earlier that evening, Kevin and I had walked around the mall—just the two of us—admiring the sparkling Christmas decorations that seemed to match our sparkling dreams of what the next day would bring.

After hanging the stockings with care, I tried to fall asleep. Similar to the night before my wedding, my thoughts would not slow down—I knew that after this night's sleep, my life would never be the same.

The days leading up to the delivery and birth of a baby are some of the most exciting couples will experience. It's likely you've already chosen your doctor or midwife and know where you will deliver the baby, whether at a hospital, a birth center, or at home.

You may have packed your bag for the hospital (for a comprehensive packing list, see Appendix VI) and created a birth plan—a document detailing your wishes for your labor and delivery. Maybe you've taken a childbirth class or watched some videos depicting the "miracle of birth." Whether you wanted to or not, you've certainly heard the stories of others by now—the empowering natural birth, the blissful epidural birth, the long labor birth, the unexpected C-section birth, the at-home-but-not-on-purpose birth.

The wide variety of childbirth experiences out there is evidence that it's impossible to predict exactly what yours will be like. And while preparation is good, all the preparation in the world will not eliminate the unknowns.

Karen Wells, a certified doula and author of *The Miracle of You: Inspirational Promises for Expectant Parents*, says, "Every component of the birth is so unknown. The best births I've seen are those where both Mom and Dad feel like they have access to everything they need—whether pharmaceutical drugs, emotional support, or just information."

THE TEAM

As you prepare for your own "D-Day," you'll want to become familiar with the "team" who will assist you through your labor and delivery. The following is a list of some of the key players.

Obstetrician or Obstetrician-Gynecologist (OB or OB-GYN)

An OB is a physician with specialized training in preconceptional counseling, the management of pregnancy, labor and delivery, and the postpartum period following childbirth. Obstetricians also receive training in gynecology, so he or she may also be referred to as an OB-GYN. An OB-GYN provides medical care to women and has particular expertise in pregnancy, childbirth, and disorders of the reproductive system. OB-GYNs who have special fellowship training in high-risk obstetrics are called maternal-fetal medicine specialists.

A majority of women who give birth in a hospital receive care from an OB or OB-GYN. This type of physician is also a good choice for women who may have risk factors, such as a serious medical condition or advanced maternal age.

Certified Nurse-Midwife or Certified Professional Midwife

Certified nurse-midwives (CNMs) receive their training as part of a master's-level nursing program and primarily perform hospital births, working under the direction of a physician.

Certified professional midwives (CPMs) receive their training by working under the supervision of another qualified home-birth midwife, either as part of an accredited school program or an accredited self-study program. CPMs are generally not permitted to work in hospitals and mainly assist at home births.

Both CNMs and CPMs must pass board examinations and adhere to stringent guidelines to ensure their ability to safely support women through labor. A midwife is a good choice if you are in good health and/or wish to deliver in a location other than the hospital. Midwives, especially CPMs, specialize in assisting with natural childbirth.[1]

Labor and Delivery Nurse

A labor and delivery nurse is a highly trained nurse specializing in obstetrical nursing. Your nurse will be assigned to you for the duration of your labor (or until her shift is over and a new nurse takes her place). Erin Smalley, a former labor and delivery nurse, says, "She will be the one who coordinates your care, advocates for what you need, monitors your progress, reports to your physician, and acts as the gatekeeper of your room."

I will never forget our long-suffering nurse, Janny (pronounced "Jenny"). As my labor was being induced—receiving Pitocin (the brand name of the drug/hormone oxytocin) in increasing amounts at thirty-minute intervals—I had to wear an electronic fetal monitor around my middle to make sure the baby was not responding negatively. Normally this would have required that I be bedridden during labor (which, in my case, would have necessitated an epidural). But honoring my wishes to labor without further interventions, Janny patiently held my monitor in place as I went through contractions.

Doula

A doula, also known as a labor coach, is a non-medical support person who assists women, their partners, and their families before, during, and after childbirth. Hired privately, the doula's role is to serve the couple throughout the childbirth experience, providing information, physical assistance, and emotional support.

Our doula helped us develop a birth plan and prepare for childbirth, and she was also present during my labor and delivery. Doulas vary in personal philosophy and education (no medical training is required to be a doula), so it's best to search for one who is qualified and shares your beliefs. (Kevin and I found our Christian doula through LinkedIn.)

God

Of course, along with your spouse, the most important member of your team is the Life-Giver Himself, who is also your ultimate Source of strength and peace. "I encourage parents to invite God into that room," Wells says. "He's always present with us, but take two minutes to pray and ask the Holy Spirit to invade that place. Acknowledge His presence; He is a part of this team."

THE OPTIONS

The options for where and how you give birth are numerous. Following are a few stories that highlight some of the common choices.

Home Birth

Ruth says she chose a home birth reluctantly because the hospitals in the town she'd just moved to didn't offer water birth as an option, which was the method she'd used when her first daughter was born. "At the office I visited, there was no guarantee that the doctor I saw for pregnancy care would be there for delivery," she says. "On delivery day, I would just have to accept whoever was working that day."

Hoping for a more personal experience, Ruth sought out a midwife and chose to give birth at home. "It's a good thing we did, because after several weeks of contractions, my water suddenly broke and my daughter was born fifteen minutes later!"

Ruth says the experience of catching her baby, placing her against her chest, and feeling her take her first breath was profound. "I was the first to touch her, the first to hold her, the first to introduce her to the world," she says. "It was beautiful!"

Because home births can carry potential risks that hospital births do not, it's extremely important that couples talk with their healthcare team and have a plan in place in the event that something unexpected happens during the labor and delivery process.

Hospital Birth with Interventions

Anna delivered all four of her babies at the same hospital, even after she and her husband moved to a town an hour away following the birth of her first. Two of her next three babies were scheduled inductions. She explains: "Because they were due in the winter, we didn't want to risk being stuck in a snowstorm on the side of the road!"

Anna says that although she went into her first labor wanting to proceed as naturally as possible, it didn't take her long to ask for an epidural when hard labor began. "In our prepared childbirth class, they had us hold an ice cube as long as we could as a way to practice breathing through the pain," she says. "Obviously, labor pains are quite different."

Speaking of her four childbirth experiences, Anna says, "I'm glad I chose the epidurals. It made childbirth a pleasant and relaxing experience—which I know goes against nature but makes me grateful for the modern times in which we live."

Hospital Birth with Limited Interventions

Callie and her husband, Devin, wanted to have "a positive, informed, natural childbirth experience," which involved hiring a doula and learning about the physiological process of labor and the effects of interventions.

After twelve hours laboring at home with techniques learned from their doula, Callie and Devin went to the hospital. Callie did not receive an epidural or pain medication. She says she felt engaged with the labor experience and shared tender moments with her husband as he supported her. "I felt so much of the Lord's presence with me while I labored," she says. "It really set Aviel's birth apart in a way that was a noticeable blessing to others."

Hospital Birth with Certified Nurse-Midwife

Beth says her commitment to natural childbirth is what led her to select a CNM for her pregnancy care. "I was initially interested in a home birth," Beth says, "but my husband (a former EMT) was not comfortable with this idea because he knew that when things go wrong, they go wrong quickly."

Beth says that along with supporting her desire to go all natural, her CNM was able to offer her more personal time than an OB-GYN could—even being with her throughout her labor at the hospital. Though Beth's medical history—which included an ectopic pregnancy and the loss of a fallopian tube—did not label her high risk, "My husband felt reassured by the fact that we would have physician backup if needed," she says.

Her unmedicated delivery went as she had hoped. She says, "My baby arrived bright-eyed, healthy, and able to nurse right away." Though Beth didn't need physician backup during labor, she's glad she gave birth in the hospital. She hemorrhaged following delivery and required medication to stop the bleeding.

Birth Center Birth
Kathleen says she and her husband, Noah, didn't choose to deliver at a birth center to "eschew modern medicine." Instead, "I wanted a natural birth because, in some primal way, it felt like the way things should be. You don't get dawn without night. You don't get Easter without Good Friday. You don't get joy without pain. I wanted to feel my baby being born."

Stages of Labor

A basic understanding of the stages of labor will help you to know what to expect.

Stage One
Early labor begins when you start having contractions that cause your cervix to efface (thin out) and dilate (open). It can be difficult to know when labor actually starts if you have been experiencing Braxton Hicks contractions (contractions that are not sufficient in intensity to dilate the cervix). Early labor can last up to a few days.

Eventually contractions will come steadily about every five minutes, last between thirty and sixty seconds, and be difficult to talk during. This is usually the time when a woman goes to the hospital. (You should also go to the hospital if your water breaks, regardless of whether or not you are having contractions. Unattended broken water can lead to infection and other complications that put the baby at risk.)

During active labor, your cervix begins to dilate more rapidly, and contractions are longer, stronger, and closer together. People often call the final stages of active labor "transition." Transition is when the most emotional stress is likely to occur. Though possibly contrary to her feelings, this is when the woman needs people around her to encourage and embolden her. Some women report becoming hostile toward their husbands or being overwhelmed with feelings of "I can't do this!" (The good news is these feelings usually precede the release of a new flood of endorphins.)

Stage Two

This stage begins when you are fully dilated (ten centimeters) and ends when your baby is born. This part of labor is called "pushing." The duration of pushing varies among women, but it generally takes longer with your first child. (I pushed for an hour and a half with my son and five minutes with my daughter.)

Stage Three

The third stage of labor begins when your baby is born and ends with the delivery of the placenta. Most women find that delivering the placenta—while uncomfortable—is quite easy after delivering the baby.

The length of labor women experience varies, but the average length of labor for a first-time mom is ten to twenty hours. Be prepared that yours may be longer or shorter.

Kathleen describes the environment of the birthing center as "warm and hospitable" with wood floors, comfy couches, and antique beds with quilts. "They were equipped with everything we needed medically," she says, "but it felt just like home." A midwife delivered the baby. "I felt like I was there with a friend," Kathleen says. "She was working right alongside me, praying with me, keeping me grounded."

When a healthy baby girl was born, Kathleen, Noah, and Baby Carolyn were able to go home four hours after the birth. "For low-risk pregnancies, I can't imagine a better way to give birth," Kathleen says. "My ideas, opinions, fears, and hopes were always heard."

THE BIRTH PLAN

A birth plan is a written document detailing your wishes for your labor, delivery, and your baby's first hours and days of life. It's a way for couples to consider all of their options and decide which are best for them. If you're giving birth at a hospital, you were probably given a form to fill out in which you can state your preferences, including:

- What comfort measures you plan on using (childbirth positions, breathing exercises, warm bath, birthing ball, epidural)
- Whether you are planning on natural childbirth or would like to receive medical interventions
- Which activities following the birth (cutting the umbilical cord, bath, trip to the nursery) you would like Dad to be involved in
- At what point your infant will be given vaccines
- If you have a boy, whether or not you would like him to be circumcised

Dr. Kevin Weary says creating a birth plan is a good idea. "A birth plan is a great way to communicate to your doctor—and especially your hospital team—your desires for what you would like labor to look like," he says. "If you have some specific preferences—like, 'I want to avoid an epidural, and it would help me if you wouldn't ask me if I want one every five minutes'—that should be discussed beforehand."

Another important function of a birth plan is allowing couples to discuss their expectations for that day and get on the same page. "The birth plan starts around the kitchen table," Dr. Weary says. "Ask, 'What do we want this to look like?' and 'What do I want my husband to do?' Talk about your expectations up front."

He emphasizes that Dad's role through labor and delivery is whatever Mom needs him to be. "That may mean holding her hand while she's pushing, helping her with breathing techniques, or yelling encouragement," he says. "She may not know what she needs until she's there, but have some ideas beforehand."

Rusty remembers watching the contractions on the fetal monitor during his wife's labor. "The line would start to go up before the contractions hit, so I could kind of tell before Karen was going to be in pain," he says. "I learned very quickly to keep my mouth shut and just support her instead of warning her when a big contraction came on."

My husband likes to tease me about the fact that I expressed great indignation whenever he suggested I "try" to do something during labor, such as breath or relax. I finally snapped, "Could you quit saying 'try'? I *am* trying!" For us, Kevin helping me to count through my breaths during contractions was more helpful than verbal "encouragement."

FLEX PLAN

If you haven't already created a birth plan and would like to, many birth plan worksheets are available online. Keep in mind that your birth plan is not an exact indicator of what will take place on the day of delivery. Hold it loosely, especially if this is your first birth.

Heather says, "With my first son, I wanted to go all natural, no drugs, and use lots of sensory things like music and candles. After laboring for fourteen hours—no playlist, just lots of moaning and groaning—I lost focus, got an epidural, and two hours later he was born." Looking back, Heather wishes she would have been more flexible with her birth plan and gotten the epidural sooner.

Dr. Weary says couples should write a birth plan but keep it in perspective. The following is a list of goals he uses with couples:

1. Our primary goal is a healthy mom and a healthy baby at the end of delivery.
2. After that, we'll try to do it just the way you want, so your delivery experience is all you were hoping it could be.
3. If that doesn't happen, we want you to at least get a vaginal birth—even if that requires interventions, such as Pitocin or even a vacuum extractor or forceps.
4. Then, if your body is simply not dilating or we're concerned for the baby, we'll do a cesarean section—and we'll do it in the interest of a healthy mom and healthy baby.
5. Ultimately, we've reached our biggest goal.

Having a smooth labor and delivery requires that you have confidence in the medical professionals overseeing your care. "It's key to establish a good relationship with your doctor during the pregnancy so you trust that they've heard you and have your best interest in mind," Dr. Weary says. "You're making yourself incredibly vulnerable to someone who's nearly a stranger. But there is a point where you need to decide, 'Am I going to trust the advice of the physician who's doing the delivery?'" (Your answer should be 'yes'.)

Dr. Weary suggests couples talk with their doctor ahead of time about less-desirable delivery outcomes, such as an emergency cesarean section, and how that will differ from a vaginal delivery. (Commonly known as a C-section, a cesarean section is a surgical procedure where an incision is made in the uterus and the baby is removed through the incision.) "For example, in many hospitals you are allowed to have many people in the delivery room, but for a C-section, only one other person is allowed," he explains. "Find out the logistics so you're not surprised."

WHEN PLANS FALL APART

When Gretta was induced with her first daughter, she hoped to give birth as naturally as possible. "My mom had three C-sections, and I *really* wanted a different story," she says.

But each time the nurse administered Pitocin, the baby would go into distress. "She was showing signs of fatigue—her heart rate would slow to that of a baby in end-stage labor, and she was just getting started," Gretta says.

After three separate tries, it became apparent they would have to take the baby by C-section. Gretta was devastated. "This was the one thing I was supposed to be able to do," she says. "I thought, *I can't even give birth.* I felt like I had failed.

"My husband was so supportive and reminded me what our childbirth teacher told us: 'Training and planning is helpful, but in the end you have to remember that the goal is a healthy baby, and you should do what it takes to reach that goal.' That really helped me focus on this story not being about me but about my baby. I wanted *her* to be healthy."

In the operating room, Gretta says her daughter was out in moments. "I remember hearing my doctor say, 'Oh, *that's* why you didn't like the contractions. The cord is around your neck one, two, three times!'"

The couple was relieved when they heard their daughter's cries and were told she was small but healthy. "I gave her a smile and a cuddle with my head," Gretta says, "and she was whisked off with the nurses and my husband for her measurements and first bath."

Bring on the Labor!

I always wondered what it would be like to go into labor. Would my water break with a splash? (This happens in only a small percentage of cases—mainly in the movies.) Would I wake up in the middle of the night with hard contractions? My questions went unanswered because I had to be induced with both of my babies.

Advice and wives' tales abound regarding naturally inducing labor. Eat some pineapple. Take a walk. Have sex. My doctor said with a wry smile that we could try all of those things, but there were no guarantees. The baby would come when he came.

Wes well remembers the days before his wife gave birth. "Nica read somewhere that intense walking can trigger the birth process," he says. "Near the end of her pregnancy, she wanted to get the party started so badly, we were taking insane hikes on really steep trails along the Mississippi River. I remember thinking, *I'm not sure I can keep up with this nine-month-pregnant woman! She's crazy!*"

When your due date is at hand, have fun trying out the "tricks." Just be sure to ask your doctor or midwife if any advice sounds questionable or unsafe. One dad reports that his wife's first labor experience was miserable after she consumed cod liver oil, which caused her to be severely ill. Fortunately, the couple went on to have six more children, with much better birth experiences.

Gretta saw her daughter again in the recovery room. "The medicine from the C-section made me pretty sick," Gretta says. "When Jay came back to the room with Kaia, he put her in my arms to hold for the first time, and I promptly threw up. I felt like such a horrible mom. Things just didn't go the way I'd planned."

Despite the detour from her own desires, Gretta sees a lasting benefit to the way things worked out. "Jay was able to hold Kaia and bond with her without interruption," she says. "He changed her first diaper, held her hand before anyone else, gave her her first kisses, and sang to her. She had five hours with her daddy. And to this day, she has a special bond with him."

Dr. Weary suggests that if the situation becomes complicated or distressing (for example, the baby isn't doing well after birth and is rushed to the NICU), parents should stay calm. "Listen to the staff," he says. "We've seen this a lot. We can tell you if it's okay. And if the baby's not doing well and we don't know why, those are the hard moments where you have to say, 'Okay, God, this is Your kid.'"

AVOIDING POSTPARTUM OPPRESSION

Jennifer DeBrito, a certified doula and author of *Expectant Parents Workshop: Devotional,* says a mom sometimes feels defeated and depressed when the birth doesn't go according to plan. She may feel as if she failed in her first task as a mom.

DeBrito uses the term "postpartum oppression" to describe a mother's urge to find her worth in her performance during childbirth or compare her experience with others. New moms make these comparisons about everything from childbirth and breast-feeding to sleep schedules and the right kind of diapers, she says.

"When you compare yourself to others, you play a dangerous game that the enemy can—and will—use against you," DeBrito explains.

"You'll end up getting tangled up in your own pride or tripping over feelings of ineptitude. Either way, you lose."

When she was preparing for the birth of her first son, DeBrito says she felt pressure to have the perfect birth plan. "I got the message that if I wanted my baby to be happy and healthy, I would need to do everything just 'right,'" she says. "In wanting to do what was best for my child, my birth plan—and my ability to stick to it—became a measure of my own worth and something I trusted instead of God."

When labor didn't go as planned and she ended up getting an epidural, she felt like a failure. "I shifted the focus of my birth plan away from God's miracle to my performance."

Karen Wells adds, "A lot of women go in with the goal to give birth naturally. I don't think that should be the goal. The goal should be to depend on God and utilize the tools available. As a parent, there are so many unknowns that you cannot plan for. The experience of childbirth, much like the experience of being a parent, is about being conformed to the image of Christ and being moved to that place where we're surrendered to His will."

∞

Kathleen says that her daughter, Carolyn, was breech until the last week of pregnancy. "We tried everything to turn her," Kathleen says. "Exercises, an excruciating procedure—it was awful." Kathleen's doctor scheduled a C-section. "I was heartbroken," she says. "I'd had my heart set on a natural delivery. Everything felt wrong."

As she and her husband prayed and sought the Lord's will, Kathleen says her heart changed. "I finally got to the place where I said, 'Okay, God. You've got this one. You know how this baby is supposed to be born. My daughter and I are in Your hands.'"

Two nights before the C-section, Kathleen and her husband were at a Bible study, and their pastor prayed for the baby and the surgery. "He prayed, 'If it be Your will, turn this baby,'" Kathleen recalls, "at which point I felt this massive lurch. Carolyn turned."

Kathleen says none of the doctors or midwives could believe what had happened. "Babies never turn that late, they said. Never." Carolyn was born naturally a week later. "I've always liked to be the one in control," Kathleen admits. "Now, slowly, I'm realizing that my Father—and my daughter's Father—is the One in charge."

BUILDING YOUR TEAM

One aspect of childbirth Grace did not expect was all the alone time she and her husband, Abe, had in the delivery room. "I was surprised by how little the nurse and doctor were around during labor," she says. "It felt like such a momentous medical thing that was happening to me, because it was my first baby, but we were alone for much of it."

Take some time to talk with your spouse about who you want "your team" to be in the delivery room. These people may include family members, such as a mother or sister, or a doula, as well as nurses and your doctor or midwife.

"You have all of these factors that are unknown," Karen Wells says. "But each person on your 'team' has a toolbox that consists of experiences as well as training that can help you."

During my own labor, my sister massaged my back and kept my ice water filled. My doula helped me with labor techniques and provided comforting Scriptures. My husband supported me physically through contractions, offered encouraging words, and prayed at each new stage of labor. And my nurse, Janny, held the fetal monitor in place during contractions. I would not have been able to remain calm and "comfortable" during labor without this team.

FIGHTING FEAR

Let's face it: Labor is scary. When I was single, I once had a dream that I was pregnant. In my dream, instead of wondering *why* I was pregnant—considering I definitely hadn't had sex—my first, panicked thought was, *This thing has to come out!*

During our preparing for childbirth class, the instructor had us place clothespins on our earlobes to simulate labor. Much like describing the Trinity, all comparative analogies fall way short of the actual thing (with the exception, I hear, of passing kidney stones). Experiencing pain like you've never felt before can create a fear response.

"Your body is being flooded with hormones—progesterone, estrogen, adrenaline, and endorphins," Wells explains. "This cocktail of hormones is driving the labor process. You're not in control."

As your brain tries to interpret what is happening, she says, it tries to put an emotion to what you're experiencing. "Active labor is very similar to a flight-or-fight scenario," she says. "Your brain goes, *The only other time I've experienced this level of adrenaline was when I almost got into that car accident.* It can make a mom feel as if there might be something wrong."

Wells says that when women can remember that their bodies are doing exactly what God created them to do, it can alleviate fear. "What's happening is normal. Childbirth is normal," she says.

I found it helpful to talk to my babies during labor, a suggestion I received from a friend. Connecting emotionally with the child I would soon meet helped me remember that the pain was worth it and something amazing was coming.

"Talking to the baby has actually been shown to lower the baby's heart rate," Wells says. "The baby is soothed by Mom's or Dad's voice. If you have any sort of complication come up, take a moment to talk to your baby, and remember that it's going to be different in eight hours, or tomorrow—and it's going to be *really* different next week."

Being aware that a miracle is taking place can make the details seem less important. "Six thousand deliveries later, I still love to tell parents, 'There's someone new in the room!'" says Dr. Weary. "What an amazing thing! If you recognize the absolute miracle that this is, suddenly the other things—the epidural you didn't want, the C-section you didn't want . . . the twelve extra hours you didn't want—become secondary."

WELCOMING BABY

And then, suddenly, it will be over. You will be holding that little one in your arms, feeling as if you've never seen anything more beautiful . . . or strange.

"When she came out, she looked like a pterodactyl," first-time dad Drew says of his infant daughter. (Don't be alarmed if a few things look different than you expected. With our daughter, it took my husband a minute to identify her gender.) Another dad compares the aftermath to something from a scene in *Criminal Minds*.

Jeff says the highlight of his wife's birth experience was holding his infant daughter. "Later, when it was just the three of us in the room, it was incredible," he says. "We were a family. She grabbed my finger, and I was in love."

During the first week, take some time to write your child's birth story (the form in Appendix VII can help). Record the details of what God accomplished in your family through your child's birth.

These are some of the words from the birth story I wrote for my son:

> As we looked forward to Josiah's birth, Kevin and I both desired that it would be an event that glorified God. I was induced at

noon. Kevin and I labored throughout the afternoon with the wonderful support of our nurse, my sister, and our doula. And at 5:56 PM Josiah Alexander entered the world. From beginning to end, God was present in the experience. During the most painful moments, I heard Him whisper: "You are My child, too. I'm taking care of you."

Welcome, sweet Josiah Alexander. Your birth honored God, as I pray your life will.

Now, it's time to take that little one home.

TIME TO TALK

- When you think about your delivery day, how do you imagine it unfolding? Write a short description or draw a picture.
- Who are the people you plan to have on "your team"? What are your expectations for the roles they'll play in the delivery room?
- List your goals for your delivery. Which goals are flexible?
- Do you feel that you have surrendered your desires for your childbirth to Christ? If you feel vulnerable to "postpartum oppression," how can you address those concerns now?
- What are some ways you can make Christ part of your delivery day?

Spend some time praying about your delivery day. Pray for your medical professionals and the other members of your team. Praise God for the ways He will work in and through you to glorify Himself as you welcome your baby into the world.

CHAPTER TWELVE

The First Few Weeks

I think one of the best things about expecting a baby is all of the preparations: Decorating the nursery. Washing tiny outfits. Arranging tiny toys.

As Kevin and I did each of these tasks together, we dreamed of the day we'd bring home our newborn son. Although we didn't know exactly what the first few weeks and months of our baby's life would be like, we already had expectations. You can probably relate.

Maybe you imagine lots of downtime as you sleep when the baby sleeps and rise for middle-of-the-night feedings. Perhaps your vision includes lots of visitors coming by to meet your little one. Or maybe Dad plans to take some time off work, and you look forward to some family time, watching movies and learning the ropes of infant care.

Everyone tells you that you can't *really* prepare for having a baby. After the excitement of the delivery wears off (and the joys of the hospital nursery no longer exist), this little being is placed completely in your care.

Jennafer, a mother of four, says, "When we had our twins, I remember being ready to go home from the hospital and thinking, *Are they just going to let us walk out of here with these babies?* I felt so unqualified and unprepared, and I thought, *Don't I have to pass a test? You have to pass a test to drive your car. I just get to walk out with these babies?*" (For more on multiples, see Appendix IV.)

It can feel a little odd and unsettling that such a huge event in your family's life is greeted with so little ceremony. The nurse goes over the infant care checklist with you, you schedule your baby's first pediatric appointment, you strap your baby into the car seat, and off you go.

Rachel recalls her first moments at home with her newborn. "I came home from the hospital, back to my warm, familiar home, put the infant car seat on the floor, cozied up to my devoted husband for a snuggle, and realized that my life was never going back to normal. There was a tiny human in that car seat. And it was 100 percent dependent on me for everything."

View from the Nursery
First Days
by Ian Durias

I think I drove home from the hospital ten miles per hour *under* the speed limit. Yellow lights were as good as red. And I was sure the speed bumps in the parking lot of our apartment complex were out to harm my newborn daughter with all that needless shaking.

I still remember those first few weeks at home with her—the softly colored wood of her crib, the Beatrix Potter decorative stickers on her wall, the blue, plush rocking chair that would lull us both to sleep.

Now, fourteen years (and four more babies) later, I laugh about how easy it was back then with only one. At the time, though, the newness of everything was a supreme challenge.

I watched a whole new side of my wife come alive. How did this woman know how to do all this stuff? Diaper changing, blanket swaddling, infant bathing . . . I sure didn't. She didn't have younger siblings growing up, she didn't babysit, and the books she read didn't cover all this stuff, did they?

I've heard it said that when people are married for a long time, over the years they'll find themselves married to six or seven different versions of their spouse. I think this is true, and I believe this is what I saw fourteen years ago—a new version of my wife, operating fully in her gifting as a mother.

I also began to discover what it meant to be a dad. I learned that love is not—and should not—be seen as an investment. To invest in something is to expect a return. When you have a baby, there's no return. There's warm spit-up on your bare shoulder, a new definition of "sleep" (or "awake"), and a line item in the budget devoted solely to diapers. What it means to be a parent is to love. Just love. Not expecting anything in return, ever.

This baby is fourteen now, and she's amazing. Creative, relational, trustworthy . . . It'd be easy to say that this is the return on loving her well over the years. I don't think that, though. Mainly because I'm nowhere near to being a perfect dad. But also because to love with an expectation holds back the love you really want to show—the love your baby needs.

WELCOME, LITTLE ONE

I remember the excitement (and slight panic) of strapping Josiah into his car seat and driving away from the hospital. Even though our townhome was minutes away, Kevin took the side streets and drove ten miles below the speed limit. Our joy was mingled with the sheer weight of the responsibility that was now upon us.

During her daughter Mykayla's first days at home, Jessica remembers sitting on the couch in the middle of the night, holding her baby close. "I would just stare at her," Jessica says. "I'd touch her tiny fingers and trace her features and just thank God that she was here and she was mine! No matter how little I slept, just staring at her perfect little face—that was half me and half my husband—would get me through another sleepless night."

I remember breathing in many of those quiet, sleepy moments with my son during the first few weeks. I would cradle his little body against my chest as we rocked or he nursed. Many times it felt as if we were in our own little world, and everything around us had slowed down or become unimportant.

Monica recalls that she and her husband, Bill, would race down the hall to be the first to reach their daughter, Isabelle, when she awoke from her nap. "That's how eager we were to see her, hold her, and love her," Monica says.

While you may be looking forward to those cuddly moments with your newborn, the transition of caring for an infant goes more smoothly for some than others.

Alysia says she had a picture in her mind of what those first days with her daughter would be like. "Once Emilyn arrived, all that went out the window," she says. "Emilyn was a fussy, colicky baby. I knew that the transition to motherhood was going to be an adjustment, but I really was not prepared for her to be screaming every waking moment and for evenings to now consist of a wailing baby that just would not calm down. I was discouraged and found myself thinking, *Was I really ready for this?*"

She says she and her husband, Chad, slowly adjusted to less sleep and figured out how to best comfort their daughter. "I started to realize that everything was going to be okay," Alysia says.

Erin Smalley says that many first-time parents feel overwhelmed when they first bring their babies home. "Having your first baby will cause many adjustments," she says. "You're going from caring for only yourself and your spouse to having a newborn fully dependent on you for his or her every need. It can feel overwhelming at times."

Alysia said it helped to shift her perspective. "I had unrealistic expectations that I would be able to just pack up my baby and take her with me," she says. "But in her first couple of months of life, we hardly left the house. I decided that life outside the home could go on the back burner. I had my precious baby now, and she would only be this small for such a short time. I just hung tight to the promise that it would get better, and I began to take it one day at a time." Now that her daughter is six months old, Alysia describes her life as "chaotically beautiful."

"I've had to learn to rely on God in a whole new way," she says. "I don't think you can ever be truly prepared for parenthood, and that is half the excitement!"

View from the Nursery
Joy, or "Just Wait"[1]
by Katie Wetherbee

As I wait in line at Target, I notice a young couple with a stroller behind me. The stroller, brand new, appears to be on its maiden voyage. I peer at the tiny sleeping newborn, his fingers curled up near his ruddy face.

"You guys do good work!" I comment. The parents beam with pride, but the weariness in their eyes lets me know that they are all still in the process of getting to know each other. The lady behind the couple glances at the stroller as well, and asks, "Is this your first?" They nod proudly. "Just wait . . ." she snorts, and then follows that with a comment about unruly teenagers.

Inwardly I wince. We seem to live in a country overrun by a great lot of negative naysayers when it comes to parenting. I remember hearing comments like that when I was a new (and overwhelmed!) mom. It seemed that many parents were suffering from a chronic case of disappointment and dissatisfaction called "Just-Wait-itis," characterized by the inflammation of impending doom in parenthood. I felt trapped in a swirl of know-it-alls who were warning me that the worst was yet to come.

Of course, now that my kids are teenagers, I know the truth. Parenting is complicated: It's wonderful and challenging; exhausting and gut wrenching; heartwarming and heartbreaking.

And, at the outset, parenting can be utterly daunting. It just doesn't help when others douse young parents with stories leading to doubt and despair.

Instead, we seasoned moms could infuse joy into our "just waits." As I regard this weary pair, I think of so many things I could say . . .

Just wait until your preschool son sees you in the hallway at pickup time and covertly grins and waves to you. (It's the best flirting in the world.)

Just wait until you watch your kindergartener jump off the bus after that first day, triumphant and tired, and melt into your arms.

Just wait until your son is up to bat and strikes out,

*holding it together despite disappointment. And just
wait until the crack of the bat meeting the ball surprises him and he races to first base . . . safe.*

*Just wait until your daughter stands up for a classmate
who is struggling, and her peers, humbled, apologize.*

*Just wait until your child, painfully tethered to
tubes and machines in the hospital, whispers, "I just
want my mommy," and you are suddenly aware that
your presence is more powerful than any prescription.*

*Just wait until your son gets his very first summer
job and he is, unmistakably, walking taller and more
confidently as a result.*

*Just wait until your child's quick sense of humor
makes you double over with laughter.*

*Just wait until you hear your son invite a friend to
church.*

*Just wait until your daughter receives her first col-
lege acceptance letter and you find yourself overcome
with tears . . . not because she's leaving, but because
she's ready.*

The baby in the stroller whimpers, breaking my reverie.
I smile at the couple and look them straight in the eye.

"You have so much joy ahead of you . . ." I remark. "Just
wait."

BEYOND EXPECTATIONS

For Rebekah and her husband, Ezra, the transition into having a baby
was fairly seamless. "It was not at all what we expected," she says, "but it

was joyful being just the three of us." Although the couple was basically on their own for the first few weeks, they preferred it that way. "We weren't exhausted from endless visitors and could really focus on what Eben needed, and we slept when he slept," Rebekah says.

Rebekah admits she and Ezra were surprised by how intense the first few weeks were. "Getting the hang of breast-feeding, cluster feeding, crying, blowouts, changing diapers—I had never even babysat, so every little detail was new," she says. "I didn't know how to change a diaper!"

Rebekah says the trials of those early days were made easier by a strong sense of teamwork with Ezra. "We really didn't have any help that first week, so we relied on each other and became a team," she says. "In the wee hours of the night, I would feed the baby, Ezra would change his diaper while I slept, and then we would repeat the process. I remember a lot of days lounging on the couch in amazement of what we had made—well, what God had made, but you get the point."

At first Rebekah says she was a little anxious about their duo becoming a trio and how that might affect their relationship. "The moment I realized I wasn't worried was during that first sleep-deprived week," she says. "I was holding our son, and Ezra whispered to me what a wonderful mom I was and how proud he was of me. I thought that to be able to love another little human, I would have to love my husband less, but that wasn't the case. Watching Ezra become a father has made me love him even more. I knew that if we could get through an exhausting pregnancy and sleepless nights with a new baby, we could get through anything that came our way, because we were in it together—all three of us."

Joshua Rogers tells new dads they should prepare to have selfish tendencies crop up. "You'll pretend to be asleep in the middle of the night when someone needs to check on the baby; you'll resent your wife for taking an hour and a half to spend with her friends; and you'll find yourself keeping score of who did what baby chore last time." He suggests that new parents confess their selfishness to Jesus and invite Him to change them from the inside out. "You'll want Him to do some magical character change in you, but instead, you'll sense the Holy Spirit saying things like, 'Hey, Buddy. Why don't you go change that nasty diaper?'"

Wes says he and his wife, Nica, came up with a creative solution to ease the pressure of early baby care. "I remember at night standing up, bouncing my daughter, trying to get her to sleep," he says. "Falling asleep standing up and bouncing. If I stopped moving for a second, she'd scream again. We took shifts for "screaming duty." But we each got one mulligan a night. We could say, 'I know it's my turn . . . but I can't do it.' And the other person would take it. It worked."

Breast-feeding: The First Big Challenge

At one of our first prenatal visits, our doctor wisely suggested we take the breast-feeding class offered at the hospital. "It's trickier than you might think," he said. "Breast-feeding can be one of the biggest challenges parents face during those first few weeks."

According to the Centers for Disease Control and Prevention, in 2010, 77 percent of women in the US breast-fed their infants for some duration. Forty-nine percent breast-fed for six months, while 27 percent breast-fed for one year (the recommendation by the American Academy of Pediatrics).[2]

And when they say, "Breast is best," they're not fooling around. Not only does breast milk contain all the vitamins and nutrients your baby needs during his or her first six months of life, it also fights disease and protects your baby from illness. Breast-fed babies suffer fewer childhood infections and viruses, and they are at lower risk for certain health problems later in life.

This protection comes from an immune system booster called secretory immunoglobulin A (IgA) found in colostrum, the first milk a woman's body produces for her baby, as well as in mature breast milk (in lower concentrations). IgA guards against germs by forming a protective layer on the mucous membranes in your baby's intestines, nose, and throat.

In addition to the health benefits for Baby, moms also experience advantages, including deeper bonding with their infants, decreased stress levels, and a lower risk of postpartum depression.[3]

Along with taking the breast-feeding class, our doctor recommended that we take advantage of the lactation services the hospital provided—both in-room following the delivery as well as support groups we could attend during the early weeks.

Hearing about the benefits of breast-feeding can understandably cause moms (and dads) to develop an obsessive desire to provide this "advantage" for their baby. Unfortunately, it's not always possible.

Grace says she fully intended to breast-feed her son. "He latched on fine," she says, "but I produced hardly any milk." After attending a lactation support group the first week after her son's birth, she learned that her milk supply was "shockingly low." Despite pumping for fifteen minutes every two hours for the next two days, Grace's milk supply did not increase.

"I remember crying all that afternoon while holding

Sam," she says. "I felt devastated that I wouldn't be able to breast-feed my son, especially when everyone made it sound so easy."

It took some time for Grace to come to terms with feeding Sam formula. "It is expensive," she says, "but how wonderful that there is such a thing as formula for babies who need it!"

She says she sometimes experienced feelings of guilt, embarrassment, and defensiveness when others asked her if she was breast-feeding. "But formula comes with a side package of freedom," she says. "A bottle means you can easily feed your baby in a restaurant, leave your baby with a sitter, and your husband can help with midnight feedings. I realized the most important thing is not that you breast-feed, but that you *have* a baby. Many women in the world would sell all their possessions in order to simply have a baby—regardless of breast-feeding."

SURVIVAL IS OKAY

Krista says the difficulty of being a new parent caught her off guard. "I always loved being with kids as a teen, and everyone used to tell me what a great mom I would be some day," she says. "That's all I ever wanted to be. It was my dream."

When her daughter was born two years after she and her husband, Craig, married, Krista was overjoyed. "The first twenty-four hours was bliss," she says. "I was so in love and running off the high of just having given birth and holding my baby for the first time. Then she started to cry at night, and we didn't know why."

The crying began at the hospital and continued when the couple took their baby home a few days later. "I'll never forget being home that first night and being completely exhausted. Craig was sound asleep—and I was upset that he got to sleep while I had to be awake with a crying baby—and I walked past the stairs of our townhouse in the middle of the night with a screaming baby in my arms.

"I glanced down the stairs and a thought crossed my mind that sent chills down my spine: *If I throw her down the stairs, she'll stop crying.* I couldn't believe that I actually had that thought, and it scared me to death. I knew I would never act on it, but the fact that the thought was even there horrified me. I woke Craig up and asked him to take over."

OB-GYN Kevin Weary says, "A screaming kid that doesn't stop screaming is difficult. The realization that 'this is hard' is okay. And there's a time when you need to walk away. You need to say, 'Tag you're it. I'm going for a walk.' Realize that you have a limit and when you're being pushed to that limit. You need to have a plan."

A plan may include placing your baby in his or her crib to "cry it out" when you need a break, or handing the baby over to your spouse and taking a short walk.

Dr. Weary likes to tell his patients a story about a night shortly after his twins were born. His wife walked into their darkened bedroom and saw their infant son lying safely on the floor, while her husband sat in the rocker.

He says he realized he needed a break and put the baby in a safe place so he could calm down. "She asked, 'What are you doing?'" Dr. Weary recalls. "And I said, 'He just needed a moment down there, and I needed a moment up here.'

"It's when people ignore their limits that they get in trouble and do something they don't want to do," he says.

Krista realized that a combination of hormones and sleep-deprivation led to her crazy thoughts. But even after her daughter, Alainna, figured out her days and nights, things didn't get better right away.

Choosing a Pediatrician

Before your baby is born, you will need to choose a pediatrician. Your pediatrician, or a doctor from his or her practice, will visit your baby in the hospital, and you will have several appointments in the days immediately following your baby's birth.

Here are three things to consider when choosing your baby's doctor:

Gather recommendations. Ask parents you know for their recommendations. Ask them *why* they like their pediatrician to make sure your priorities are similar.

Research. In addition to finding out your doctor's credentials, look into the office's policies on vaccinations, hours of operation, and after-hours care. Our pediatrician's office provides emergency care until 8:00 PM on weeknights, weekend hours, and a twenty-four-hour nurse line—services that give us greater peace of mind.

Interview. Plan to interview at least two pediatricians. Kevin and I only interviewed the top recommendation we received, which didn't allow us to consider other options. While we liked the doctor, not doing our homework necessitated a switch later on when the practice didn't meet our needs.

Remember that different parents gravitate toward different doctors. Many of our friends chose doctors based on relaxed vaccination policies and style of care. Kevin and I discovered that because we ourselves are laid-back, we prefer a more proactive doctor, one who acts quickly and decisively.

"She was a baby, which meant a lot was required of me," Krista says. "I resented a lot of the things I had to give up for her, such as the freedom to do what I want when I want. I resented Craig for still seeming so 'free.' Here I was living my 'dream' and instead living in a world of resentment. I would find myself going through the motions of the day and feeling distant from my baby.

"I did have plenty of moments of bliss. But I was caught off guard by the survival mode I found myself in. So many moments would slip by, and I'd think, *This is all I ever wanted. Why am I not happy? Why can't I thoroughly enjoy this?*"

Krista says there was no magical cure to her new-baby blues. Instead, "God gave me moment-by-moment grace. I looked for joy, I prayed for delight, and I begged for patience. God gave me just what I needed, but I was a surviving-in-the-moment mom."

Krista now has four children, and her youngest is four. "Clara was my redo," she says of her youngest child, who came five years after the first three. "I found so much intense joy and delight in her because I realize how fleeting it is. They aren't in diapers forever; eventually you *do* sleep through the night on an extremely regular basis, everyone can go potty on their own, buckle their own seat belts, and read their own books."

POSTPARTUM DEPRESSION

Jerusha Clark, author of *Living Beyond Postpartum Depression,* says she was trying to do everything "right" following the birth of her first daughter. She was running on a daily basis, eating healthy foods, and breast-feeding. She even had the opportunity to take a vacation to Hawaii when her daughter was six weeks old. "I felt like I was one of the lucky ones," she says.

But when her daughter was three months old, Clark's milk supply dried up unexpectedly. As feelings of inadequacy overwhelmed her, she was thrown into a downward spiral of anxiety and depression. In her book she writes:

> A suffocating sense of failure and disappointment haunted me. . . . Though I didn't realize it at the time, my feelings of inadequacy and anxiety extended far beyond breast-feeding.[5]

Feelings of failure led to sleepless nights, weight loss, and tears that wouldn't stop—and eventually thoughts of harming herself and her baby. After a frightening trip to the ER and three days in a mental health facility, Clark began treatment for her severe postpartum depression (PPD). Once she started taking medication prescribed by the doctor and began receiving counseling from a marriage and family therapist, Clark began to improve. Within eight weeks she felt like herself again.

But six months after the birth of her second daughter, it happened again. Her milk supply dried up, initiating the vicious cycle that once again led to PPD. This time she was proactive and went back on antidepressants when she felt the sadness creeping in, but when she was feeling a little better, she stopped taking them without consulting her doctor.

The depression returned worse than before, and this time she nearly took her own life. God spared her, but Clark says she had a difficult time coming to terms with the fact that it had all happened again. Still, God faithfully led her to the medical, spiritual, and emotional help she needed to recover, and she pulled out of the darkest season of her life.

According to *The Complete Guide to Baby and Child Care,* between 5 and 10 percent of women experience postpartum depression, which seems to be brought on by the changes in hormone levels that occur after pregnancy. Though there is no single cause for PPD, biological, emotional, and lifestyle factors may all play a role.

PPD can begin anytime during the first six months after child-birth. A mother with PPD may be so intensely depressed that she has difficulty caring for her baby, or she may develop extreme and unreal-istic anxiety over the infant's health.[6]

Dr. Weary says it's normal for new mothers to feel overwhelmed. "The combination of exhaustion, changing hormones, sleepless nights, the stress of a new baby—that's just a drastic, tough combination of hard things," he says. "But if you're having a hard time finding anything good, or you feel like, 'I'm going down this dark drain and can't seem to pull out,' you need to talk with someone."

(For more information on coping with postpartum depression, see Appendix III.)

BABY BLUES

Between 50 and 60 percent of women are affected by a lesser form of postpartum depression called "baby blues." This common mood problem usually begins during the first week after delivery. According to *The Complete Guide to Baby and Child Care*:

> Symptoms can include irritability, tearfulness, anxiety, insomnia, lack of energy, loss of appetite, and difficulty concentrating.[7]

Unlike postpartum depression, baby blues is a temporary physical and emotional slump, caused by hormonal changes following child-birth, and it usually fades away in two to three weeks.

My friend Kelsey, a pastor's wife, remembers triumphantly taking her daughter to church three days after she was born. But the follow-ing Monday, when her mother-in-law called to ask how she was doing,

Kelsey says, "I started to say, 'I'm fine . . .' but only got out 'I'm fi—' before I burst into tears. I was so exhausted and overwhelmed. Within ten minutes she was at my house folding my laundry. I took a long nap, and it was just what I needed!"

The best remedy for baby blues is making sure you have plenty of support, eating and drinking regularly, and getting plenty of rest. But if depression persists for longer than three weeks or your symptoms worsen, you should consult your doctor.

LONG DAYS, SHORT YEARS

The first days of your child's life may be some of your hardest, but they will also be some of your most precious. More importantly, they won't last forever.

Ashley says she remembers lying on the floor of her son's room when he was two weeks old and thinking, *Oh my goodness. I will never be able to undo this. I am stuck for the rest of my life with a child.* "I was already mourning the loss of (what I thought was) my awesome no-kid life," she says. Today her son is two and a half. "Now I think, *Oh my goodness. I only have a little time with this cute, wonderful human being.* I would never ever want to go back to my life before him. Ever."

Parenting, like marriage, often gets even better with time. Author Gary Thomas recently became an empty nester. "You need to have a long-term view of parenthood," he says. He compares parenting to a marathon, where not all the training is fun, but the satisfaction is great.

"It's when the marathon is over that you look back and see that the pain was a part of the fun," he says. "It doesn't feel fun, but when you look back, those will be really good years."

The years go fast, Thomas says, and it's easy to take them for granted in the midst of being tired and having greater responsibility.

Still, he says, if God offered him the chance to have his children young again for just one weekend at the price of $10,000, he'd pay it.

"Watching your children grow is one of the greatest joys in life," he says. "I can't describe the feeling I had when my son made it to the state cross-country meet. He was once a little boy in diapers and a toddler running around the house. Now, he'd set a goal and achieved it. It was amazing."

Thomas says that parenting also brings new joy and meaning to the marriage relationship. "People love romantic thrills, but I can't describe how meaningful it is when you can sit together and watch God work in the lives of your children. It's meaningful because you both love them so much."

Thomas says that although there are many things he and his wife, Lisa, would do differently in their early parenting, they take satisfaction in raising their children in a home that stayed together.

"All my family books have *sacred* in the title," Thomas says. "Sacred means you protect it. You protect your kids' home by protecting the marriage. You decide: *This is going to be a citadel. We're going to create this safe, sacred space, and we're going to defend it.* It really is miraculous that God allows us to live in families. It's a precious, precious thing."

Someone has said of parenting, "The days are long, but the years are short."[8] Never is that truer than during the early days of your child's life. So go ahead—prepare for some sleepless nights and demanding days. But that's not all. Get ready for something else—some of the best years of your life.

TIME TO TALK

- What do you imagine your first week with the baby to be like? Talk through some potential stresses with your spouse.

- What are your plans for feeding your baby? What sources of support are available if you are planning to breast-feed?
- What challenges do you anticipate during your first few weeks of parenting?
- What is your plan for when you've reached your emotional limit?
- What are some ways you can you embrace a "long-term view of parenting," as Gary Thomas suggests?

Reflect on what you would like your first week home with the baby to be like. Pray that you will feel God's peace and presence during your first week of parenting and beyond. Thank Him for the blessing of being a family.

ACKNOWLEDGMENTS

I would like to thank my family—my husband, Kevin, and my little ones—for their love and encouragement as I pursue my passion for writing in the midst of a busy season of our lives.

I would also like to thank my parents for being faithful to the Lord and to one another, allowing me to experience the joys and benefits of being part of a family established in the Lord. Your love, support, and humor have given me a firm foundation. Thank you, also, to my siblings, Matthew, Sarah, and Rebekah, for cheering me on and being lifelong friends.

I would like to thank my parents-in-law. You have been such a sweet blessing and encouragement to me through your generous offerings of childcare, baby clothes, meals, fellowship, and so many other kindnesses. I feel blessed to be part of your family.

Thank you to the parenting team at Focus on the Family for dreaming up a book for couples just beginning the adventure of parenthood and for entrusting me with your vision. And thank you to the editorial team, and specifically my editor, Brandy Bruce, for patiently and skillfully coaching me through the process of writing my first book. I couldn't have had a better experience.

Thank you to friends, and new friends, who opened your hearts and told your stories. This book would not be possible without you; your stories *are* changing lives.

And most of all, I thank my Lord and Savior, Jesus Christ, who brings light into the darkness and gives life. Your goodness and love amaze me. May this book be a sacrifice of praise to You.

We Named Her Noah

by Ashleigh Kittle Slater

We named her Noah. I will never forget her.

News of her death came at my ten-week OB appointment. I woke up that fateful Wednesday to the thought, *Today your life is going to change.* Two hours later, it did. A Doppler ultrasound (a test using reflected sound waves to estimate blood flow through blood vessels, including those in an unborn baby) failed to detect a heartbeat; an ultrasound revealed a body much smaller than my due date required. The doctor estimated she had stopped growing at five weeks gestation.

For five weeks—thirty-five days—I was unaware that I was a walking tomb. I avoided caffeine, exercised with care, and jotted down lists of potential baby names, not knowing her tiny body had ceased to grow within mine.

A week after my D&C (dilation and curettage—a surgical procedure in which the cervix is dilated and a special instrument is used to scrape the uterine lining), a friend asked my husband, Ted, "How's Ashleigh doing? Is she getting over it?"

I wasn't.

Life felt as if it played out in a bad dream, a nightmare from which I longed to wake up. I wept, paced, and had to force myself to climb out of bed and to eat. At times, anger overwhelmed me.

And then I hit resigned.

Resigned was worse than numbness; worse than a pillow wet with tears. It was the acceptance that this was just the way it was, and there was nothing I could do to change it. It was realizing that we wouldn't have a baby on or near Ted's birthday, and that, when Christmas came, there wouldn't be four smiling kids on our card. It was a place where the comfort of weeping came to me less often.

But in the early weeks, the scariest moments were the ones where I felt better. Because, in those moments when the sadness wasn't so bad, I felt disloyal to Noah.

THE AMPUTEE

I'm not alone in struggling with feelings of disloyalty. My friend Amy, who lost a baby several years ago, told me, "I know just what you mean about feeling disloyal. We moved across the country, from Indiana to California, six months after my miscarriage. I felt very disloyal, as though I were leaving my child there. When I became pregnant again after losing the baby, I felt disloyal to be excited."

And Angie Smith, whose daughter Audrey died two and a half hours after her birth, writes in her book *I Will Carry You: The Sacred Dance of Grief and Joy*:

> The process of healing has been winding and unpredictable to me. One day I'm starting to feel like myself again, and even that can make me feel guilty sometimes. I don't feel like I have a right to be normal.[1]

The truth is, there is no such thing as "normal" after the death of a baby. There is, as my friend Jennifer—whose sister and yet-to-be-born nephew died in a car accident six years ago—points out, a "new normal." She shared with me:

> From my experiences there isn't really a moving on . . . but
> a new "reality," a new normal. . . . I think you will gradually
> "acclimate" to your circumstances, but there will be a lingering
> of what would have been. . . . You will think of how old Noah
> would be and what you imagine her to be doing.

In *A Grief Observed,* C. S. Lewis's journal-turned-classic work, he captures well this new reality Jennifer speaks of:

> To say the patient is getting over it after an operation for appendicitis is one thing; after he's had his leg cut off it is quite another. After that operation either the wounded stump heals or the man dies. If he heals, the fierce, continuous pain will stop. Presently, he'll get back his strength and be able to stump about on his wooden leg. He has "got over it." But he will probably have recurrent pains in the stump all his life, and perhaps pretty bad ones; and he will always be a one-legged man. There will be hardly any moment when he forgets it. Bathing, dressing, sitting down and getting back up again, even lying in bed, will all be different. His whole way of life will be changed. . . . At present I am learning to get about on crutches. Perhaps I shall presently be given a wooden leg. But I shall never be a biped again.[2]

I've come to understand that Noah's death is not something I'll "get over." Her short life and untimely death are ingrained into who I am. It's something, as Lewis points to, with which I have to learn to live.

But as an amputee, as Lewis now labels me, I have a choice about how I will live with it. What will my "new reality" or "new normal" look like? Will I equate a depressed state with loyalty to Noah and her memory? Will I feel guilty in those moments when the sorrow isn't as strong? Or will I choose to honor her life with what some have labeled "bright sadness"?

BRIGHT SADNESS

Jenny Schroedel, in her article titled "Rachel's Tears," describes this term *bright sadness* as "a kind of 'bitter joy' or 'joyful mourning.'"[3] To the logical mind, this figure of speech is an oxymoron. Pairing the contradicting emotions of "sorrow" and "joy" together simply doesn't make sense to the rational mind. But as I, and many others who have walked through grief, have learned, these two antonyms can and do coexist. The joy doesn't negate the sadness; rather, it mingles with it. The two dance, as Angie Smith writes.

For me, bright sadness has come after slowly and painfully wading through the raw emotions of grief. I simply had to walk through this anguish first. And the truth is, when the pinhole light of joy began to shine into my sorrow, I didn't know what to do with it, except accept it as a gift from God.

As I've started to make sense of and embrace this "joyful mourning," I'm seeing that I can honor Noah through it. As I mourned the baby I will never hold in my arms, the bright sadness that accompanied me brought with it a hopeful reminder: Noah is not lost. She isn't abandoned to the cold ground of a cemetery. Her spirit is alive and well in the presence of a strong, tender, compassionate Savior. While my arms may not hold her, His do.

We named her Noah, our child who ushered me into this season of bright sadness. I will never forget her.[4]

APPENDIX II:
EXPECTANT THROUGH ADOPTION

A Different Kind of Birth

by Erin Smalley

Three and a half years have passed, but I remember it like it was yesterday.

After months of filling out forms, completing checklists, and going through background checks, our family of five had traveled across the world to welcome three-year-old Antoinette Rose into our family.

Despite our thorough preparation, I remained nervous about many things. *How am I going to feel? Did I remember to bring everything I need? How will she respond to us?*

Questions swirled in my mind. We lingered in Nanchang, China, along with other families, awaiting the knock at the hotel door that would signal the expansion of our families through adoption.

We carefully arranged everything in the room—the crib, blankets, toys, clothing, diapers. I had tears in my eyes as I took a moment to stand back and reflect on the scene—a scene that felt oddly familiar to me. All at once, I realized it was very much like preparing for the arrivals of our biological children.

Then came the knock on the door. Precious Annie was greeted with cheers, smiles, and celebration of her arrival. She took one look at us and sprinted down the hotel hallway to escape the chaos. After we retrieved her, I attempted to do my best to comfort her—feeling so much like I did with each of my newborns—fumbling my way through figuring out what she needed or wanted.

As an adopted child myself, I remember my mom telling me, "God brought you to me all the way from the other side of North Dakota," while her other children were "just born." I smile now at that memory, knowing it was her way of making me feel extra special. But the truth in her words is that we all arrive in our families through different modes—adoption being one wonderful method God uses to bring families together.

If you are currently awaiting a child, I know you are feeling many different emotions—anticipation, uncertainty, joy—maybe all of them at the same time. As we awaited Annie's arrival, I had moments of action, moments of questioning, and moments of great joy. In so many ways, the experience was similar to the emotions I felt as I awaited the deliveries of our three biological children. Once each little one was born, I felt like I needed to get to know this new little person.

Annie was no different. The first night she was in our room, I slept near her crib, and I woke up over and over again to make sure she was still breathing. Although she was in a much bigger body, it brought back many memories. And, like the little girl who was once "brought all the way from the other side of North Dakota," Annie was brought to our family—by God—from the other side of the world.

APPENDIX III:
SURVIVING POSTPARTUM DEPRESSION

———ᗄᑐ———

Jerusha Clark, author of *Living Beyond Postpartum Depression*, says that PPD caught her unaware. "I assumed that it wouldn't happen to me," says the mother of two. "I think a lot of Christian women are in that place because many have fulfilling marriages, feel ready to have a baby, and may not have struggled with depression in the past. I was so desperate to be a good mom, I didn't recognize that what I was dealing with was something that I couldn't just 'try harder' to overcome."

Clark offers these suggestions for moms who experience postpartum depression:

Listen to the counsel of others. I was so eager to prove myself as a good mom that I wasn't willing to listen to my husband. Listen to your husband, parents, siblings, and close friends who notice you're different. Be willing to listen even if it feels like someone is attacking you.

Remember that it's treatable. Statistics show that only one-third of women who are depressed get treatment; of the third who get treated, most have significant turnarounds between six and eight weeks.

Resist believing the enemy's lies. I felt that God was punishing me for things I did in my past, specifically the eating disorder I'd struggled with in high school. Women with PPD may think, *I deserve this. I had sex before I got married. I had an abortion. I didn't want the baby at first. God must be punishing me.* All of these accusing thoughts come from the enemy. These thoughts do not come from Christ.

Seek physical, emotional, and spiritual treatment. PPD is never caused by just one factor. Even something that's happening physically can have an emotional component. With my first daughter, I had a traumatic delivery that ended in an emergency C-section. That played a role in how I started out in my parenting experience. Our brains are so intricate that our spirits and our emotions and our biology are intertwined. This is an opportunity—just like all suffering—to draw closer to God.

APPENDIX IV: MULTIPLES

Motherhood Times Two

"I always laugh when people say, 'You got two for the price of one,' says Jennafer, the mother of twins. "I don't know if I would say that." With her hormone levels twice that of a woman carrying a single baby, Jennafer describes her pregnancy as "rough."

She experienced a condition called hyperemesis gravidarum (HG) that caused her to vomit regularly from the sixth week of pregnancy until her babies were born. "I dropped fifteen pounds from not keeping anything down," she says. "Then I gained it back plus fifty pounds more."

Jennafer recalls a time when her husband, an OB-GYN who had seen hundreds of pregnant women, actually gasped when she turned around and he saw her pregnant belly. (She suggests that husbands *not* gasp at their wife's appearance if at all possible.)

When her twins were born, a boy and a girl, she said caring for them was intense. "Sometimes I longed to have just one little baby that I could hold and feed and have fall asleep in my arms," she says. "Other times I felt like a milk factory."

Out of necessity, she and her husband, Kevin, developed a teamwork approach to parenting. "While I would nurse one, Kevin would burp the other," she says. "Sometimes he'd ask, 'Which one do I have?'"

The couple made it through the double parenting intensity of caring for two babies, and when they were four years old, Jennafer became pregnant again. "The day I went in for my first ultrasound, I was feeling sick and had to lie down on the bed," she says. "I thought, *This is feeling awfully familiar* . . ." At that moment, she says the Lord impressed on her heart words from 2 Corinthians 12:9: "My grace is sufficient for you." This prepared her for the news she would receive at the ultrasound appointment—they were having another set of twins, this time two boys.

"We cried," she says. "Then for two years we didn't leave our house except to drive the babies around."

She says she and Kevin depended on each other and the help and encouragement of others because they had no choice. Now with two thirteen-year-olds and two nine-year-olds, Jennafer says they have no regrets. It may have been four for *the price of four,* but the price was worth it.

APPENDIX V:
ADDING A BABY TO
YOUR BLENDED FAMILY

Ron Deal, author, therapist, and expert on blended families, says that sometimes a couple with children from a previous marriage may feel some concerns when adding a mutual child to the family—what some call an "ours" baby.

In *The Smart Stepfamily: Seven Steps to a Healthy Family,* he writes:[1]

Stepfamilies experience a wide variety of emotional and relational changes after a mutual child is born. When relationships within the home are generally stable and positive before the pregnancy, the mutual child has a greater chance of bringing a positive impact to the home. In fact, half-siblings may consider the mutual child a full sibling, which can bring a great sense of joy to everyone.

If the relationships within the stepfamily home are already divided, a mutual child can bring further division. The biblical account of Joseph and his half-brothers is an example of this dynamic, Deal says. Stepparents can create a smoother transition by continuing to invest in their stepchildren as well as their biological children. In addition, parents should be aware of the unique pressures their baby will face. Deal writes:

Being related to everyone puts the mutual child in the center of the family's experience. This hub position cuts both ways. On the one hand, it is a privileged position, and the child gains more attention than the other children (especially part-time children). This affords the child more influence and control in the home. On the other hand, this child may feel a constant pressure to create bonds between family members and ensure that everyone gets along.

The families who fare best, Deal explains, are the ones where the husband and wife are united on household standards and committed to the fair treatment of all of their children.

> Parental unity is a must to negotiate the rules and standards of the home, and all children should be treated equitably to the best of your ability. A stepparent, for example, should not disconnect from stepchildren to give themselves exclusively to their biological children. Some differences will exist, but the extremes should be avoided at all costs.

Deal suggests discussing the changes ahead with all of your children, talking about how the schedule may change or how some (natural) jealousy may arise. He also recommends including siblings in the excitement of welcoming the baby as much as possible—establishing that every family member is valued and loved.

It's also important for parents not to assume that every frustration a sibling expresses over the new baby is automatically a "stepfamily problem." In *The Smart Stepmom,* he writes:

> Sibling rivalry is normal. Not every expression is "stepfamily rejection." And if a stepmom overreacts it sends a rejecting message to the children in return.[2]

The entrance of your new baby can be a joyous event for the whole family with a little preparation, sensitivity, and family togetherness.

APPENDIX VI: PACKING YOUR HOSPITAL BAG

The Super-Duper Comprehensive Hospital Bag List

One thing Kevin and I enjoyed doing in the weeks leading up to our son's birth was packing our hospital bag. Here are the things that we (and a few of our closest friends) found most useful:

For labor:
- Hair ties
- Warm socks or slippers
- Flip-flops
- iPad with birthing playlist
- DVDs of favorite movies
- Tennis ball (for back labor)
- Chapstick
- Toothpaste
- Toothbrush
- Deodorant
- Gum or mints (fresh breath is a must!)
- Camera/video camera
- Bible

For recovery:
- Robe
- Shampoo
- Nursing bras (take two)
- Nursing shirts
- Your own loose-fitting clothing (or maternity clothes you wore at six months)
- Favorite treat (apple pie was one recommendation)

For baby:
- Car seat (install the base before you go)
- Baby's first outfit

Also take along anything that will make you feel more comfortable. Some additional suggestions: air mattress (for dad), your own pillow, and soft maternity pajamas.

APPENDIX VII: BIRTH STORY

Recording Your Child's Birth Story[1]

Use this form to remember and celebrate the details of your baby's birth.

The birth story of _____

Date and time of birth: _____

Who was present? _____
_____

What we were doing when labor started: _____
_____
_____

How labor progressed: _____
_____
_____

What Mom remembers most: _____
_____

What Dad remembers most: _____
_____

When we prayed and what we prayed for: _____

_____

_____

Scriptures we used: _____

_____

_____

How God answered our prayers: _____

_____

_____

Measures we used for comfort: _____

_____

_____

Anything else we want to remember: _____

_____

_____

_____

_____

_____

(Adapted from *Expectant Parents Devotional: Workshop* by Jennifer DeBrito. Used by permission.)

APPENDIX VIII:
LOSING BABY WEIGHT

Bye-Bye Baby Weight

Every mom wants to look good after pregnancy. I remember how I savored each utterance along the lines of, "Wow! You don't look like you just had a baby." (No matter that I had exerted maximum force to button those jeans and was wearing a strategic black T-shirt to hide the muffin top.)

When the time comes to drop the weight—six to eight weeks following the birth for most women—start off slowly. Remember that if you are breast-feeding, you still need to be consuming an additional 500 calories a day. And if you're working out, you also need to replace those calories. The American College of Obstetricians and Gynecologists (ACOG) suggests no more than one pound of weight loss per week while breast-feeding.

Here's how a few moms said good-bye to the baby weight:

After giving birth to three boys in four years, I had gone from my pre-pregnancy weight of 140 to almost 200 pounds, the heaviest I had been in my life. As a stay-at-home mom, I was tired all the time. I decided to make a change. I joined a gym and found a time when my husband could watch our boys each day. Four days a week I took classes I enjoyed. The gym is the best for me because I need to be motivated by other people.

I also changed my diet to include filling foods that were

lower in calories. I lost sixty pounds in nine months, and I've kept it off for over a year. I feel better, have more energy to play with my boys, and am more sane because I get some time to myself.

—Min

My friend, who had a baby a few weeks before I did, started a sixty-day challenge group for moms trying to lose weight. We communicate on Facebook and encourage each other to eat healthfully and work out consistently.

Being new mothers, there's no condemnation when one of us is up all night with a baby and skips a workout. Losing weight has made me feel a lot more like myself—like I'm getting back a part of me, and focusing on part of my life that's not all about the baby.

—Jennifer

I developed a thyroid disorder during my pregnancy and rapidly put on more than fifty pounds; only nine came off when my son was born. Despite following a strict diet and taking high doses of expensive medication, the weight wouldn't budge. One of my girlfriends, a mom of eight, started a low-glycemic eating plan and had so much success that I was inspired to try it as well.

After three months of having level blood sugar, I was down to the minimum dosage of thyroid medication, had much more energy, and had lost twenty-nine pounds.

—Jaime

NOTES

Chapter One

1. Robert Epstein, "What Makes a Good Parent?" *Scientific American Mind*, November/December 2010, 46–51.

2. Joshua Rogers, "A New Father, a Better Husband," *Meeting God in Real Life* (blog), July 26, 2011, accessed May 16, 2014, http://joshuarogers.com/2011/07/26/a-new-father-a-better-husband.

3. Gary Thomas, *Devotions for a Sacred Marriage: A Year of Weekly Devotions for Couples* (Grand Rapids: Zondervan, 2005), 41.

Chapter Two

1. "FAQ: General Questions," CountTheKicks.org, accessed May 16, 2014, http://www.countthekicks.org/faq; and "Fetal Movement: Feeling Your Baby Kick," Baby Center, http://www.babycenter.com/0_fetal-movement-feeling-your-baby-kick_2872.bc.

2. Jennifer Bly, adapted from "What Husbands Can Do for Their Pregnant Wives," *The Deliberate Mom*, February 3, 2011, http://thedeliberatemom.com/what-husbands-can-do-for-their-pregnant-wives/.

Chapter Three

1. Ava Neyer, "I Read All the Baby Sleep Books," *Huff Post Parents* (blog), April 23, 2013, http://www.huffingtonpost.com/ava-neyer/i-read-all-the-baby-sleep-advice-books_b_3143253.html.

2. Linda Sharps, "Frustrated Mom's Hilarious Take on Conflicting Sleep Advice for Babies Is a Must-Read," *The Stir* (blog), April 24, 2013, accessed May 16, 2014, http://thestir.cafemom.com/baby/154616/frustrated_moms_hilarious_take_on.

3. Tony Evans and Chrystal Evans Hurst, *Kingdom Woman* (Colorado Springs: Tyndale/Focus on the Family, 2013).

4. Rebecca Stone, "When He Speaks: Part 1," *With Pen in Hand* (blog), July 20, 2013, accessed May 16, 2014, http://beccawithpeninhand.blogspot.com/2013/07/when-he-speaks.html.

5. Stone, "When He Speaks: Part 2," July 23, 2013, accessed May 16, 2014, http://beccawithpeninhand.blogspot.com/2013/07/when-he-speaks-part-2.html.

6. Catherine Claire Larson, "Embrace the High Calling of Parenthood," *Catherine Claire Larson's Blog*, May 20, 2013, accessed May 16, 2014, http://www.goodreads.com/author_blog_posts/4230 214-embrace-the-high-calling-of-parenthood.

Chapter Four

1. Stephanie Pappas, "The Science of Dad: Engaged Fathers Help Kids Flourish," LiveScience, June 13, 2013, http://www.livescience .com/37435-fathers-importance-kids.html.

2. Kim Parker and Wendy Wang, *Modern Parenthood: Roles of Moms and Dads Converge as They Balance Work and Family* (Washington, DC: Pew Research Center, 2013), 6, 27–28, http://www.pewsocialtrends .org/files/2013/03/FINAL_modern_parenthood_03-2013.pdf.

3. David Popenoe, *Life without Father* (New York: Free Press, 1996), 163, cited in Jeffrey Rosenberg and W. Bradford Wilcox, *The Importance of Fathers in the Healthy Development of Children* (Washington, DC: US Department of Health and Human Services, 2006), 11, http://www.childwelfare.gov/pubs/usermanuals /fatherhood/fatherhood.pdf.

4. Rosenberg and Wilcox, *The Importance of Fathers*, chap. 2, http:// www.childwelfare.gov/pubs/usermanuals/fatherhood/fatherhood .pdf.

5. Randy Alcorn, "Incredible Privilege of Fatherhood," Eternal Perspective Ministries, February 22, 2010, http://www.epm.org /resources/2010/Feb/22/incredible-privilege-fatherhood.

6. Joshua Rogers, "How to Forget Your Spouse Is Wonderful," *Meeting God in Real Life* (blog), October 18, 2011, http://joshuarogers .com/2011/10/18/how-to-forget-your-spouse-is-wonderful.

Chapter Five

1. US Department of Labor, Bureau of Labor Statistics, "Employment Characteristics of Families Summary—2013," news release, No. USLD-14-0658, April 25, 2014, http://www.bls.gov/news .release/pdf/famee.pdf.

2. Philip Bump, "The American Family Is Leaning In to Working Moms More Than Ever," *The Wire*, May 29, 2013, http://www.theatlantic wire.com/national/2013/05/working-moms-poll-pew/65690.

3. US Census Bureau, "One-Third of Fathers with Working Wives Regularly Care for Their Children, Census Bureau Reports," news release, December 5, 2011, https://www.census.gov/newsroom /releases/archives/children/cb11-198.html.

4. National Bureau of Economic Research, "Business Cycle Dating Committee, National Bureau of Economic Research," September 20, 2010, http://www.nber.org/cycles/sept2010.html.

5. Wendy Wang, Kim Parker, and Paul Taylor, *Breadwinner Moms* (Washington, DC: Pew Research Center, 2013), 12, http:// www.pewsocialtrends.org/files/2013/05/Breadwinner_moms _final.pdf.

6. US Census Bureau, "One-Third of Fathers with Working Wives Regularly Care for Their Children," https://www.census.gov /newsroom/releases/archives/children/cb11-198.html.

7. Dennis Cauchon, "An American Role-Reversal: Women the New Breadwinners," *USA Today*, March 25, 2013, http://www.usa today.com/story/news/nation/2013/03/24/female-breadwinners /2015559.

8. Kimberly Eddy, "The Accidental Housewife," *Boundless*, September 22, 2010, http://www.boundless.org/adulthood/2010 /the-accidental-housewife.

9. Sheryl Sandberg, *Lean In* (New York: Random House, 2013).

Chapter Six

1. Kelly Wallace, "Hands Off! Rubbing Pregnant Bellies Might Be Illegal," CNN.com, "CNN Parents," November 6, 2013, http:// www.cnn.com/2013/10/28/living/parents-illegal-touching -pregnant-belly.

2. Lydia E. Harris, *Preparing My Heart for Grandparenting* (Chattanooga: AMG Publishers, 2010).

3. Erin Davis, "How to Live with, and Love, Your Mother-in-Law," *True Woman* (blog), June 1, 2011, accessed May 16, 2014, http:// www.truewoman.com/?id=1713.

4. Matt Walsh, "You Don't 'Lose Your Freedom' When You Have Kids," *The Matt Walsh Blog*, October 5, 2013, accessed May 16, 2014, http://themattwalshblog.com/2013/10/05/an-uncensored -true-tale-of-parenting.

Chapter Seven

1. American Pregnancy Association, "Miscarriage," http://american pregnancy.org/pregnancycomplications/miscarriage.html (last accessed May 30, 2014).
2. Katie Wetherbee, *Diving for Pearls* (blog), http://katiewetherbee.com.

Chapter Nine

1. Robert Epstein, "What Makes a Good Parent?" *Scientific American Mind*, November/December 2010, 46–51.

Chapter Ten

1. Mike Spohr, "31 Things No One Tells You about Becoming a Parent," BuzzFeed, November 25, 2013, accessed May 16, 2014, http://www.buzzfeed.com/mikespohr/what-no-one-tells-you-about -becoming-a-parent.

Chapter Eleven

1. For information on choosing a midwife, apprenticing practical midwife Jennifer Green recommends "Choosing a certified nurse-midwife," Baby Center, accessed May 16, 2014, http://www .babycenter.com/0_choosing-a-certified-nurse-midwife_322.bc.

Chapter Twelve

1. Katie Wetherbee, "Joy, or 'Just Wait?' " *Diving for Pearls* (blog), February 26, 2012, accessed May 16, 2014, http://katiewetherbee .com/2012/02/06/joy-or-just-wait.
2. National Center for Chronic Disease Prevention and Health Promotion, Breastfeeding Report Card: United States/2013 (Atlanta: Centers for Disease Control and Prevention, 2013), 2, http://www .cdc.gov/breastfeeding/pdf/2013BreastfeedingReportCard.pdf.
3. American Academy of Pediatrics, "Executive Summary: Breastfeeding and the Use of Human Milk," 2012, http://www2.aap.org /breastfeeding/files/pdf/Breastfeeding2012ExecSum.pdf; "How Breastfeeding Benefits You and Your Baby," Baby Center, http:// www.babycenter.com/0_how-breastfeeding-benefits-you-and-your -baby_8910.bc?page=3.
4. American Academy of Pediatrics, "How to Choose a Pediatrician," HealthyChildren.org, 2010, accessed May 16, 2014, http://www

.healthychildren.org/english/family-life/health-management/pages/How-To-Choose-A-Pediatrician.aspx.

5. Jerusha Clark, *Living Beyond Postpartum Depression: Help and Hope for the Hurting Mom and Those Around Her* (Colorado Springs: NavPress, 2010), 17.

6. Paul C. Reisser, *The Complete Guide to Baby and Child Care* (Carol Stream, IL: Tyndale, 1997), 109–111.

7. Ibid., 109.

8. Gretchen Rubin, *The Happiness Project: Or Why I Spent a Year Trying to Sing in the Morning, Clean My Closets, Fight Right, Read Aristotle, and Generally Have More Fun* (New York: HarperCollins, 2009).

Appendix One

1. Angie Smith, *I Will Carry You: The Sacred Dance of Grief and Joy* (Nashville: B&H Books, 2010), 135.

2. C. S. Lewis, *A Grief Observed* (New York: HarperCollins, 1961), 52–53.

3. Jenny Schroedel, "Rachel's Tears," *Jenny Schroedel* (blog), November 17, 2005, accessed May 16, 2014, http://jenschroedel.com/2005/11/rachels-tears.

4. Adapted from Ashleigh Kittle Slater, "We Named Her Noah," *Ungrind* (webzine), June 1, 2010, accessed May 16, 2014, http://ungrind.org/2010/we-named-her-noah.

Appendix Five

1. Ron L. Deal, *The Smart Stepfamily: Seven Steps to a Healthy Family* (Minneapolis: Bethany House, 2006), [Need page #].

2. Ron L. Deal and Laura Petherbridge, *The Smart Stepmom: Practical Steps to Help You Thrive!* (Minneapolis: Bethany House, 2009), 250–52.

Appendix Seven

1. Jennifer DeBrito, *Expectant Parents Workshop Devotional* (CreateSpace Independent Publishing, 2013), Kindle ebook. Used by permission.

The Family project™
A Divine Reflection

INTRODUCING THE GROUNDBREAKING FOLLOW-UP
TO FOCUS ON THE FAMILY'S THE TRUTH PROJECT®

THE PROFOUND IMPACT OF BIBLICAL FAMILIES

From the creators of the life-changing series *Focus on the Family's The Truth Project* comes a stunning, new journey of discovery that explores family as a revelation of God—and the extraordinary impact families have on the world around them. Introducing *The Family Project*, a transformative feature-length documentary and DVD small-group experience that reveals—through an in-depth exploration of God's design and purpose— biblical truths about the role of families in society.

VISIT
FamilyProject.com
TO LEARN MORE

A PROGRAM OF FOCUS ON THE FAMILY®

Your
Journey to
Parenthood
Extends Beyond this Book

What you do for family
is what they'll do for life.

IT STARTS WITH YOU.

GEN3™ starts with a promise—a commitment to be a thriving family for three generations.

By making intentional decisions every day, you can share a lasting legacy with future generations.

What you do for family is what they'll do for life.

FocusOnTheFamily.com/Gen3

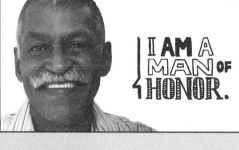

MAKE THE GEN3 PROMISE.